THE DEAD SEA SCROLLS

THEIR MYSTERIES AND HISTORY REVEALED

JOHN DESALVO PhD

SHELTER HARBOR PRESS
NEW YORK

This 2014 edition published by Shelter Harbor Press by arrangement with Alexian Limited

Text Credits
Scripture quotations taken from the **Holy Bible, New International Version**. Copyright © 1973, 1978, 1984 by International Bible Society.
Used by permission of Hodder & Stoughton Publishers, A member of the Hachette Livre UK Group. All rights reserved. "NIV" is a registered
trademark of International Bible Society. UK trademark number 1448790. **Josephus The Complete Works** Copyright translated by Willian
Whiston © 1998 Thomas Nelson Publishers. **Pliny the Elder Natural History: A Selection** Copyright © 1991 John F Healy, Penguin Group.
The Dead Sea Scrolls A New Translation Copyright © 1996 Michael Wise, Martin Abegg, J R & Edward Cook, HarperCollins Publishers

Pict ure Credits
AKG Images, London 27 Jean Lou-Nou, 67 Museo del Prado/Madrid, 72 Erich Lessing/Israel Museum, Jerusalem, 83 Udo Hesse,
104 Erich Lessing, 105 + 106 Peter Connolly, 116 and 121R Erich Lessing/Archaeological Museum/Amman, 136 Jean Louis-Nou/
Archaeological Museum/Amman, 147 Erich Lessing/Archaeological Museum/Amman
Courtesy of Judith Anne Brown/John Allegro Estate and Jan Irvin www.johnallegro.org 142, 143
Cameron Collection 12 British Library, 18, 21 British Library, 54, 80, 91, 114, 117, 160
Corbis, London 07 Richard T Nowitz, 69 Nathan Benn, 70 Bettmann, 78 Hulton-Deutsch Collection, 146, 187 Ted Speigel,
188/189 Jim Hollander/epa,
Dr John C Trever, PH.D/Corbis 37, 39 , 59, 90, 177
Bruce E Zuckerman/West Semitic Research/Dead Sea Scrolls Foundation/Corbis 55, 65, 71, 138
Les Stone/Sygma/Corbis 48, 75, 76/77
Jeffrey Markowitz/Sygma/Corbis 62, 63, 82, 88
Gettyimages, London 9 David Rubinger/Time Life Pictures , 13, Kenneth Garrett/National Geographic, 31+ 46 Express/Hulton Archive ,
38, Three Lions/Hulton Archive, 43 David Rubinger/Time Life Pictures , 49 Fred Mayer, 73R Normand Blouin/AFP, 74 Al Fenn/Times Life Pictures, 81Kenneth Garrett/National Geographic, 92 Ecole Nationale Superieure des Beaux-Arts,Paris /Bridgeman Art Library, 99 Harvey Lloyd/Taxi, 100 Menahem Kahana/AFP, 134 David Silverman, 150 Salah Malkawi, 151 Mark Kauffman/Time Life Pictures , 161 Stephane de Sakutin, 164 Vatican City Museums and Galleries/Bridgeman Art Library, 169 Pushkin Museum,Moscow/Bridgeman Art Library, 176 Menahem Kahana/AFP, 178/179 National Gallery. London/Bridgeman Art Library
Jupiter Corporation Images 22, 23, 33, 60, 62 + 94, 98, 101, 111, 113, 139, 157, 159, 166 187 NASA 32
The John Rylands University Library/University of Manchester 23 St Johns Fragment recto P RYL. 9K 457 PC 11 + 20, 14, 15, 16, 17, 19, 20, 24/25, 26, 28, 29, 40, 41, 42, 56, 57, 61, 64, 86, 93, 95, 102, 110, 115, 122, 135, 140, 141both, 145,
149, 153, 154, 155, 156, 158 both, 162, 163, 167, 173, 174, 175
Zev Radovan www.BibleLandPictures.com 34, 35, 36, 44, 45, 46, 47, 52, 53, 55, 66, 79, 87, 89, 97, 103, 107, 108, 109, 119, 120, 121,
124, 125, 126, 127, 128, 129, 130/131, 133, 137, 144

Cataloging-in-Publication Data has been applied for and may be obtained from the Library of Congress.

Shelter Harbor Press
603 W. 115th Street
Suite 163
New York, NY 10025

ISBN: 978-1-62795-006-0

Printed and bound in Thailand

10 9 8 7 6 5 4 3 2 1

Contents

Foreword

The Dead Sea Scrolls are considered to be one of the major archeological finds of the twentieth century. These scrolls are more than just ancient or dead manuscripts; they can give new meaning to our lives and our beliefs. They can even give us new insights into the time when Jesus lived and help us to understand much about how both Christianity, which was in its infancy when they are thought to have been written, and Judaism, have evolved. Since their discovery in 1947, the scrolls have elicited much research, discussion, and debate. The world's top scholars and researchers have studied these scrolls and there is still controversy surrounding them today. Many questions remain unanswered.

A common misconception is that the Dead Sea Scrolls are the oldest surviving religious literature in the world. In actuality, the Pyramid Texts from ancient Egypt are the oldest, dating from approximately 2650 B.C. Though not the oldest, the Dead Sea Scrolls may, however, be the most significant religious texts ever found. Almost all experts now agree that they were written sometime between 250 B.C. and A.D. 70. This period would overlap with the lifetime of Jesus Christ (estimated 4 B.C. to A.D. 33) and, needless to say, the value of these scrolls to Christianity and Judaism is therefore enormous.

Although they were discovered in 1947, it was not until 1991 that all of the scrolls and fragments were made available to researchers and to the public. During the time they were kept

▲ A conservator restoring a fragment of an original scroll. Except during restoration work, the scrolls are preserved behind glass in a temperature-controlled environment.

private, they were the most guarded and protected manuscripts in the world. Now we have the benefit of studying all of them to see what they reveal. The significance of this is that the Dead Sea Scrolls are not reserved just for scholars, but are available to everyone. Since the 1990s a portion of the scrolls and fragments has been exhibited in some of the world's major cities, drawing huge interest from the general public. Numerous books and television specials have featured the Dead Sea Scrolls and just about everyone today has heard of them, although most individuals may not know much about their details. Today, new research and new controversies have also emerged.

Issues that are important not only to the biblical archeologist but also to the average person are how the information of the scrolls changes or confirms our understanding of the Bible, both the Old and New Testaments, and whether there are any new ideas in the Dead Sea Scrolls regarding current religious beliefs of either Christians or Jews. Information on these and other issues contained in the Dead Sea Scrolls may have a personal impact on many.

When the news about the discovery of the Dead Sea Scrolls was released to the public, there was considerable apprehension about what the scrolls might reveal. Could these scrolls have a radical effect on Christianity and even on Judaism? Would these scrolls challenge the authority of the Bible? Would the Dead Sea Scrolls be a new Bible that would replace the old one or would it supplement it and fill in some of the historical gaps? Would it show that the Bible has changed very little during its history? These were some of the questions that many were asking at that time. So, besides the excitement of this amazing archeological find, there was also much anxiety about what it could mean for our current religious beliefs and practices. Unfortunately, these questions would have to wait until the scrolls and fragments were assembled and translated. Today, this process is almost complete and, although there are many fragments that still need to be put together, the majority of the important scrolls and fragments have been assembled and translated. We can now look at some of these questions and discuss what the Dead Sea Scrolls may mean to religious ideas today.

One of the most exciting discoveries about the Dead Sea Scrolls is that they contain new and previously unheard-of stories about known biblical personalities, such as Noah, Abraham, and Enoch. There are stories that are not in the Bible that claim to be authored by Moses, as well as new prophecies that no one has ever heard of before. A very fascinating area is that the Dead Sea Scrolls discuss the apocalyptic end times and the Antichrist. It would be very interesting to compare this scenario with the one described in the book of Revelation. Now that these new prophetic sections have finally seen the light of day it will be interesting to see how well they fit with our current beliefs.

Other areas of scroll texts, and which I like to classify as mystical or magical texts, concern divination and astrology. There are also texts concerning angels. The finding of this type of text opens up new questions regarding the beliefs and practices of Judaism and early Christianity. Were divination, astrology, angelic invocations, and magic accepted forms of religious practice at that time?

It is important to note that what are known as the Dead Sea Scrolls are held within large amounts of textual material. Experts believe that originally there were over 800 complete texts; in fact, some believe almost 900, which made up the original Dead Sea Scrolls before many were damaged, destroyed, or lost. A few complete scrolls have been recovered and some partial scrolls, but most are only fragments of a text, some no bigger than a fingernail. In fact, for some texts, we have only one small fragment from that scroll. It may seem incredible that from just one small fragment experts can deduce that this was part of a larger individual scroll. There are tens of thousands of fragments that were recovered and the job of putting these together is astronomical. The work goes on, and as more fragments are fitted together to form the text, we learn more about what the authors of the Dead Sea Scrolls were trying to tell us.

One of the most interesting discoveries has been the similarity between the beliefs of the writers of these scrolls and early Christianity, such as the belief in the coming of a Messiah, ritual baptism, common property, and end time apocalyptic views. These and other similarities are further explored, since they raise some very interesting questions about who actually wrote the scrolls. There is even a Dead Sea Scroll about a Pierced Messiah.

The Dead Sea Scrolls continue to draw attention, cause controversies, and mystify academics and the general public alike. That there are more discoveries to be made is beyond doubt; and that many will be able to gain new insight into our spiritual beliefs and practices through reading them is also certain.

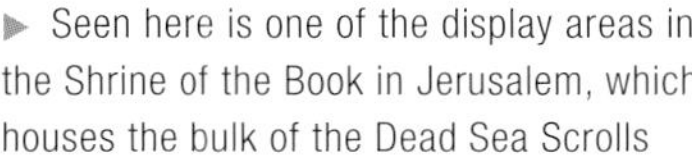

▶ Seen here is one of the display areas in the Shrine of the Book in Jerusalem, which houses the bulk of the Dead Sea Scrolls

1 Ancient Religious Texts

THE DEAD SEA SCROLLS REPRESENT THE MOST RECENT ADDITION TO THE BODY OF JUDEO-CHRISTIAN SACRED TEXTS, WHICH THEMSELVES FORM PART OF A LARGER GROUP OF RELIGIOUS TEXTS DATING BACK THOUSANDS OF YEARS.

ואין מחריד׃ יככה יהוה
בשחין מצרים ובעפלים
ובגרב ובחרס אשר לא
תוכל להרפא׃ יככה יהוה
בשגעון ובעורון ובתמהון
לבב׃ והיית ממשש בצהרים
כאשר ימשש העור
באפלה ולא תצליח את
דרכיך והיית אך עשוק
וגזול כל הימים ואין מושיע׃
אשה תארש ואיש אחר
ישגלנה בית תבנה ולא
תשב בו כרם תטע ולא
תחללנו׃ שורך טבוח
לעיניך ולא תאכל ממנו
חמרך גזול מלפניך ולא
ישוב לך צאנך נתנות
לאיביך ואין לך מושיע׃
בניך ובנתיך נתנים לעם
אחר ועיניך ראות וכלות
אליהם כל היום ואין לאל
ידך׃ פרי אדמתך וכל יגיעך
יאכל עם אשר לא ידעת
והיית רק עשוק ורצוץ
כל הימים׃ והיית משגע
ממראה עיניך אשר תראה׃
יככה יהוה בשחין רע על
הברכים ועל השקים

Introduction

It is important when considering the Dead Sea Scrolls to fit them into a chronological framework and so understand how their dates of composition align with the writings of other known religious and sacred literature. We will start by examining some of the most important and ancient religious texts known. It is also important to keep in mind that the date of the physical writing of any text may be much later than the time it was first composed or created, as it is most likely that it would have originated as an oral teaching passed down from one generation to the next. Eventually, someone or some group would have recorded it in writing. In actuality, an ancient discovered text may have been recorded hundreds or even thousands of years later than its oral tradition began. For example, most biblical scholars believe that the oral tradition stories about Jesus in the Gospels began after Jesus died (A.D. 30s), and were most likely to have been first written down sometime between A.D. 70 and 90. The oldest New Testament

▲ A conservator working on a sample of the Judas Gospel discovered in 1978 in Egypt.

◄ A page from the Diamond Sutra, a Tang dynasty Buddhist text found in Dunhuang, China and dating from the ninth century B.C.

fragment ever found has been dated to A.D. 125.

So we must distinguish these dates when we discuss the different texts. Dates given must be the date the text is thought to have been first orally composed, or the date it is thought it was first written down, or the date of the oldest surviving fragment of this text we currently possess. Archeologists and historians, through much research and extrapolation, may be able to estimate the date when certain texts were first composed and first written down, but this is certainly an educated guess. On the other hand, we can determine fairly accurately the dates of the actual physical texts that we have in our possession using a variety of dating techniques.

Pyramid Texts

The Egyptian Pyramid Texts are the oldest known religious or sacred writings that we know of in the world. These texts were found carved on the inner walls and chambers of several pyramids at Saqqara in Egypt. They were also carved on the stone coffins or sarcophagi inside these pyramids. Egyptologists believe they were written during the Old Kingdom period around 2650 to 2175 B.C. (This is different from the Book of the Dead which evolved from the Pyramid Texts later, during the Middle Kingdom period.) Even though they were written in the pyramids during this period, many archeologists believe they were actually composed much earlier, in about 3000 B.C. The texts consist of spells and directions for guiding the deceased pharaoh through his journey in the afterlife. They discuss how he could travel, especially by flying in his spirit body, and also contain spells for him to use to call the gods to help him.

▶ The Pyramid of Teti I, seen here, has all but disappeared, although the interior remains remarkably intact.

The oldest of all the written Pyramid Texts are thought to be the texts from the pyramid of Unas, and these contain over 200 spells. The texts in the pyramid of Unas were written during the fifth dynasty; later texts from the sixth dynasty were found in the pyramids for King Pepi I and II.

▲ Texts carved on the interior wall of the Pyramid of Teti in Saqqara.

Gaston Maspero, a French Egyptologist, discovered the Pyramid Texts in 1881. Samuel Mercer published the first complete translations in 1952. This was followed by an excellent translation by R. O. Faulkner in 1969. About 760 spells from all the pyramids have been recorded and published.

"The Book of the Dead" would more accurately be entitled "The Book of the Coming Forth by Day". The title "The Book of the Dead" was coined by Karl Richard Lepsius, a German Egyptologist who published some of the texts in 1842 and gave them this name.

▲ A vignette from The Book of the Dead of Nesmin, depicting the tribunal of Osiris, was painted on papyrus between 525 and 332 B.C.

Like the Pyramid Texts, The Book of the Dead is a later collection of spells and procedures written to help the dead in the afterlife. It is thought that they were composed between 1600–1200 B.C. and it was customary to place copies of the spells and procedures written on leather or papyrus with the dead. They have also been inscribed on pyramids, tombs, and sarcophagi (stone coffins). It appears that the Pyramid Texts were sources and primary material for composing the Book of the Dead; however, unlike the Pyramid Texts, these were not just for the exclusive use of the pharaoh but also for the common man or woman. Almost one third of the chapters come from, or are derived from, the Pyramid Texts. With the evolution of the Book of the Dead, the average Egyptian could have these texts painted or inscribed on his or her tomb or coffin and have his own manual for the afterlife. One famous Egyptian theme in the Book of the Dead which many have heard of is the "weighing of the heart." In this story, the deceased person's heart is weighed against a feather to judge the person's character. If his heart weighs less than the feather, he is found righteous, joins the company of the gods, and has passed the test. If, on the other hand, the heart weighs more than the feather, he fails and is devoured by a monster, and his existence ends. Over time, the original Pyramid Texts evolved into the Book of the Dead.

Vedas

These texts are the oldest texts of the Hindu religion in India and were written in Sanskrit. They consist of hymns, mantras, incantations, rituals, and other religious teachings. The Hindus believe that they were divinely revealed to mankind; that is, they were not composed by man but directly revealed from God. Some orthodox groups accepted this claim of divine authorship but others denied it. These other groups separated from the orthodox and formed their own religions which we now know as Buddhism and Jainism. There are four Vedas: The Rig, The Yajur, The Sama, and The Atharva. The Rig Veda is the oldest of the four and is considered to have been composed around 1500–1300 B.C. Scholars believe it was committed to writing between 300–200 B.C.

◀ A 19th century copy of the Rig Veda manuscript, the oldest of the four Vedic texts.

Enuma Elish

The Enuma Elish is the Mesopotamian story of creation, which predates the Old Testament story of the creation in Genesis, and was discovered in the library of Ashurbanipal located at Nineveh. The story was first translated and published in 1876 by George Smith. It was written in Akkadian on seven clay tablets using cuneiform script. A blunt reed, known as a stylus, was used to make this script on clay tablets. This script was one of the earliest known forms of writing created by the Sumerians around 3000 B.C. These tablets were discovered in 1849 and are considered to date from 1300–1100 B.C., but were probably composed much earlier, in about the 18th century B.C. This discovery was very significant as it revealed to scholars a clear understanding of how the Babylonians viewed creation. It tells the story of how mankind exists for the service of the gods. It also tells about the chief god Marduk, and how he is supreme among all the Mesopotamian gods. The title Enuma Elish translates to "When on High." There has been much debate and discussion about whether the Hebrew Bible story of creation was based on the Mesopotamian story, which predated it, or on a common source that was used by both. This is a controversial issue and has still not been resolved, but there are many similarities between the two stories and also many important differences. In both stories, the creation is based on the word of God or the act of divine speech by a god. However, in the Genesis story in the Bible, there is one God rather than many, and He does not act frivolously like the gods in the Enuma Elish story.

▼ A 19th century depiction of what Nineveh may have looked like during its heyday and showing the Ashurbanipal library where the Enuma Elish tablet was kept.

◀ One of the clay tablets on which Enuma Elish, the Mesopotamian story of creation, was written.

Old Testament or the Hebrew Scriptures

The Hebrew scriptures known as the Old Testament are considered to have been composed between the 12th and second centuries B.C. They were mostly written in Hebrew, with a few Aramaic sections, and were composed by many authors during this period. Up to the time of the discovery of the Dead Sea Scrolls, the oldest copies or fragments known about were from medieval times. These fragments, which were written around A.D. 950, are known as the Aleppo Codex. The far older Dead Sea Scrolls not only contain text from every book of the Old Testament with the exception of the book of Esther, but also contain stories not included in the Bible.

▼ Fragments of the Old Testament written around A.D. 950 and known as the Aleppo Codex.

The Bhagavad Gita

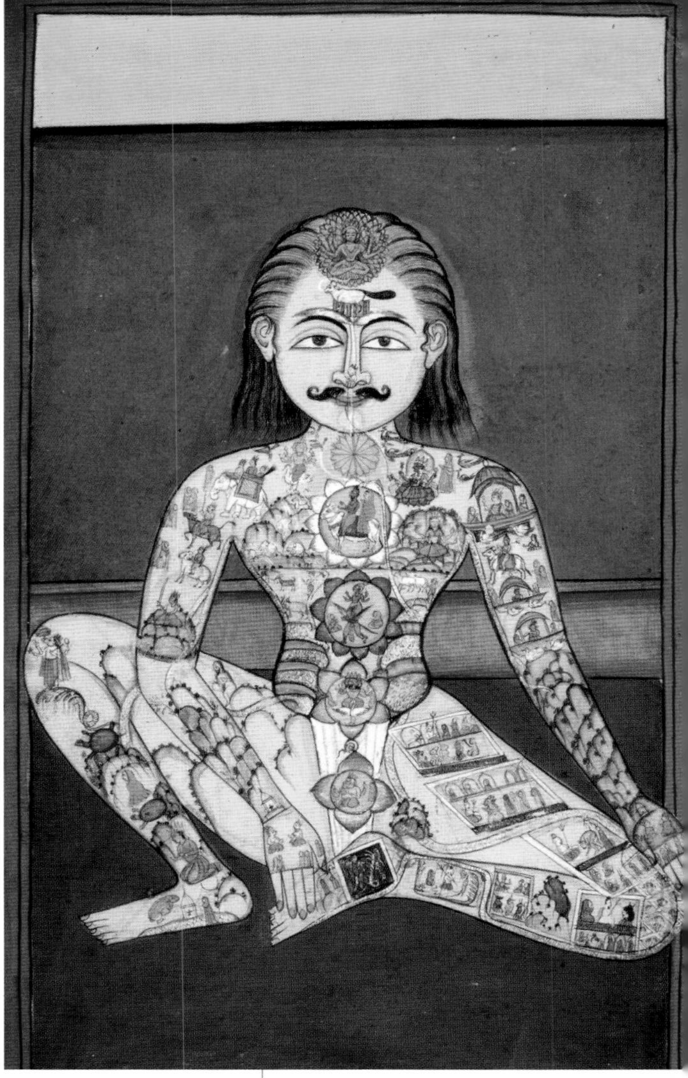

The Bhagavad Gita is the main sacred text of the Hindus and is believed to date from around 300 B.C. It is basically a dialog between Arjuna, a warrior, and the god Krishna. This dialog takes place just before the battle at Kurukshetra. It appears that Arjuna has a moral dilemma about fighting this major battle. Krishna reassures him that it is his duty to fight this battle since he is a warrior and prince of the people. He explains this using teachings and philosophies to justify Arjuna's role as a warrior and his duty on the battlefield. It gives the reader insights into life and its problems, and is considered a sacred Hindu teaching text. Eventually, Krishna reveals himself to Arjuna as the Supreme God and gives him a vision of his Divine form. There are deep meanings and philosophical teachings throughout this sacred text and it is the most sacred text of the Hindu religion.

▲ Yoga is a spiritual practice, designed to overcome selfishness and attachment to the world, and is a key teaching contained in the Bhagavad Gita.

Yoga is discussed in the Bhagavad Gita as a system to produce a unified and peaceful mind. Suffering and misery on earth is caused by the ego, or selfishness, and by attachment to the world. The discipline of quieting the mind is necessary to overcome this selfishness, and detachment is necessary to overcome suffering and to be united to God. Yoga helps one to be detached but in tune with the will of God.

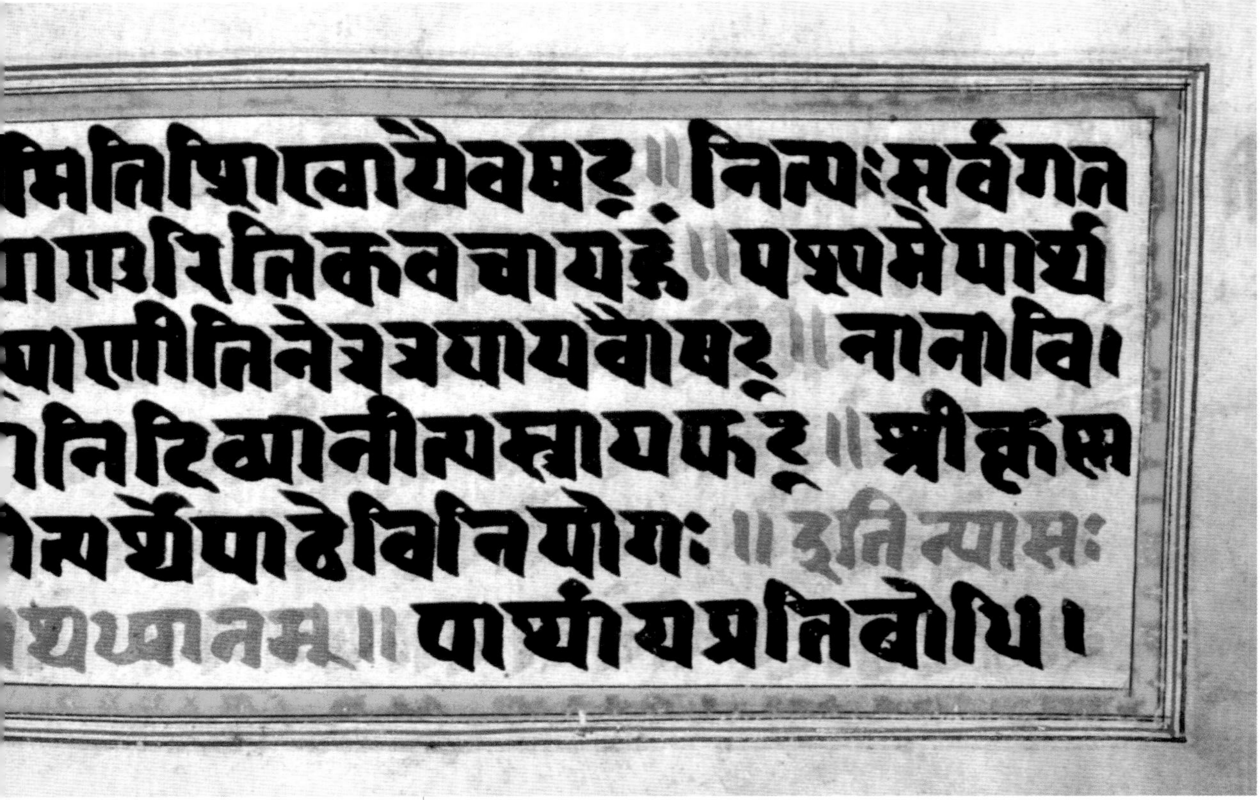

▲ An 18th century copy of the Bhagavad Gita, a core Hindu text originally written in Sanskrit.

There are three types of Yoga: the yoga of devotion, known as Bhakti Yoga, the yoga of selfless action, known as Karma Yoga, and the yoga of self-transcending knowledge, known as Jnana Yoga. These three different techniques or paths lead to the same goal. The goal of life is to escape the wheel of births and deaths (reincarnation) and to attain the god-consciousness or nirvana.

Dead Sea Scrolls

The Dead Sea Scrolls, believed to have been written between 200 B.C. and A.D. 68, are written in three different languages, Hebrew, Greek, and Aramaic. They are the oldest known Bible manuscripts in existence.

New Testament

The John Rylands fragment is considered to be the oldest known manuscript fragment of the New Testament. The New Testament, or the scriptures of the Christians, is considered to have been written in about A.D. 70–90, and is mostly written in Greek. The fragment known as the Rylands fragment is a papyrus fragment that is believed to have been written between A.D. 125–150. There is not complete agreement on this date range, with some scholars assigning it a date in the second half of the second century A.D. The fragment measures only 3.5 by 2.5 inches. It has seven lines of writing on each side and contains, in Greek, parts of the Gospel of John, (Jn. 18:31–33 on the front and Jn. 18:37–38 on the back). It was discovered in Egypt in the 1920s and the first translation was completed in 1943 by C. H. Roberts. It is currently in the John Rylands Library in Manchester, England.

◄ The John Rylands Fragment. Text is written in dark ink on papyrus and is still legible, many centuries after it was written.

Nag Hammadi

Many people confuse the Dead Sea Scrolls with the Nag Hammadi, but these texts are completely different, not only were they found in a different location but also they were written at a different time. The Nag Hammadi texts were buried in the desert in Egypt and found accidentally in 1945, and are named after the location of their discovery. Sealed in a jar and buried for almost 1,500 years, the texts are 12 papyrus codices, written in Coptic, containing 52 treatises considered to be the texts of the Gnostic sect. These manuscripts date from the third century and one of the most famous is the Gospel of Thomas. They are considered to be one of the most important archeological finds of the twentieth century. The Gnostics, who produced them, lived in the first and second century A.D. and

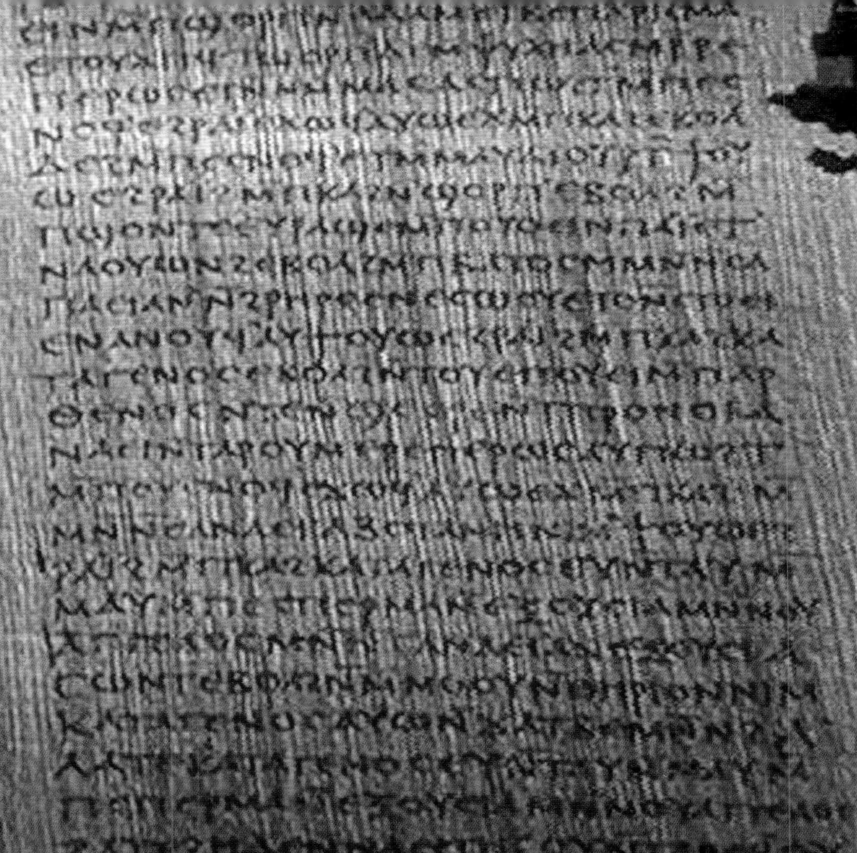

◀ Two folios of the Nag Hammadi, which deal with Gnostic philosophy, which prevailed in Alexandria in the first century A.D.

the actual writing of the texts has been dated as A.D. 100–200. Also known as the Gnostic Gospels, they are a collection of early Christian Gnostic texts written in Coptic.

The story of their discovery is fascinating. In December 1945 two Egyptian brothers were digging for fertilizer near Habra Dom in Upper Egypt. While digging, they came upon a large vessel, which they dug up and decided to break open. At first they were scared that it might contain an evil spirit but the thought of finding treasure in the jar helped them to overcome that fear. Sadly, while the manuscripts were in the family's possession, the boys' mother burned several manuscripts as firewood but, fortunately, the majority of the manuscripts were recovered. They are now housed in the Coptic museum in Cairo, and have helped to shed much light both on the Christianity of that time and on the beliefs of the Gnostic sect.

The Qur'an

The Qur'an is the central religious text of the Muslims. It was written in Arabic in the seventh century A.D. and is considered to be the words of Allah revealed to the prophet Muhammad through the Angel Gabriel. It consists of 11 chapters, and each one is called a Sura. The title for each chapter was given by God. It is thought that Muhammad could neither read nor write, but that he recited what God told him and his words were written down by one of his companions. Muslims believe that the Qur'an is sacred scripture and they use it as their guide to living.

The Qur'an did not exist as a single book in Muhammad's lifetime. Several hundred years after his death, a caliph collected all the existing fragments and traditions of available material and they were assembled into one book. This was then distributed to other places and as Islam expanded, in about A.D. 650, a standard version was produced.

سورة الفاتحة الكتاب
بسم الله الرحمن الرحيم
الحمد لله رب العالمين الرحمن الرحيم
مالك يوم الدين إياك نعبد وإياك نستعين
اهدنا الصراط المستقيم صراط الذين أنعمت
عليهم غير المغضوب عليهم ولا الضالين
وهي سبع آيات مدنية

▶ A Qur'an, dating from A.D. 1200, which was once owned by the sultan Abd al-Aziz Khan.

▶ Opposite: Verses from Sutra 11 of the Koran, written if Kufic and carved in stone.

بسم الله الرحمن الرحيم
الله لا اله الا هو الحي القيوم
لا تاخذه سنة ولا نوم له ما
في السموت وما في الارض من
ذا الذي يشفع عنده الا باذنه
يعلم ما بين ايديهم وما خلفهم
ولا يحيطون بشيء من علمه الا
بما شاء وسع كرسيه السموت
والارض ولا يوده حفظهما
وهو العلي العظيم

Han Dynasty Mawangdui Scrolls

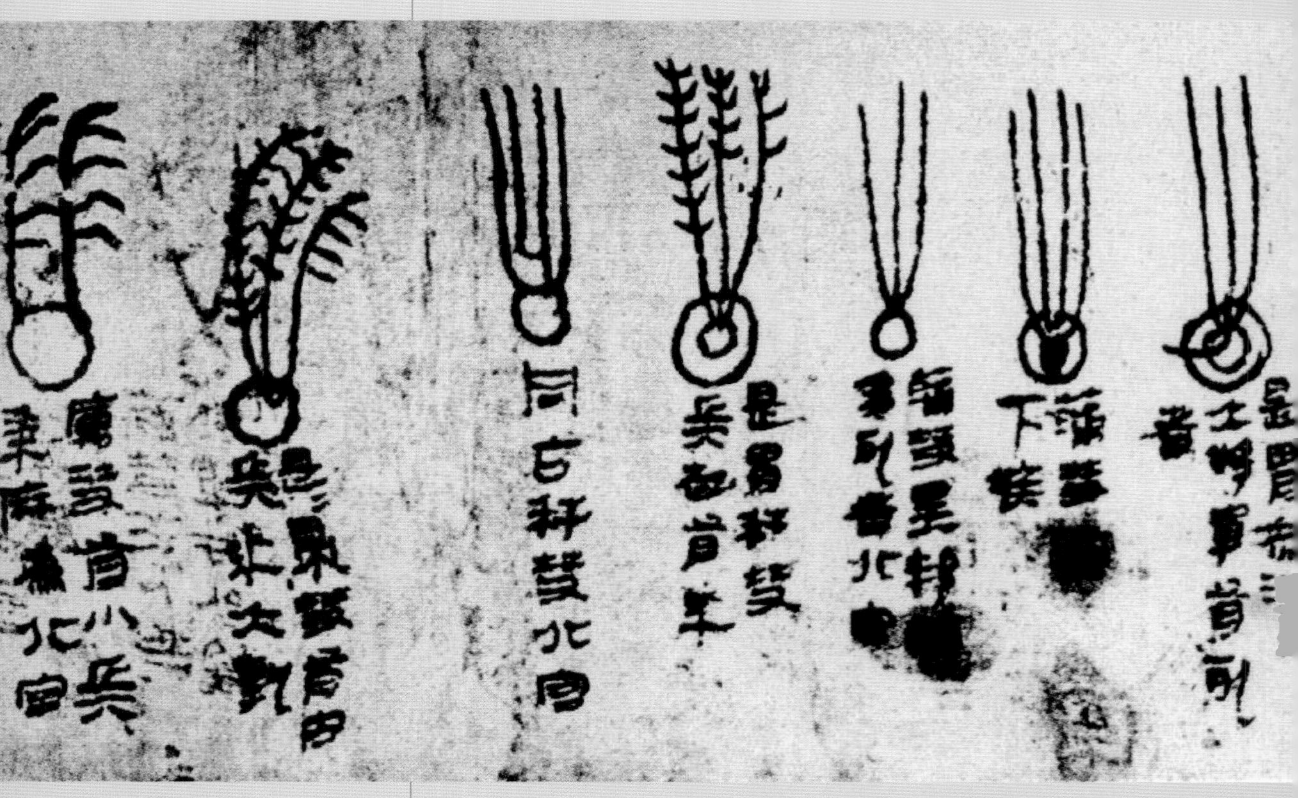

▲ One of the Mawangdui scrolls which, in the section illustrated, talks of comets and their movements.

Mawangdui is an archeological site near the town of Changsha in the Hunan province of China. In the 1970s, three tombs were uncovered dating back to the second century B.C. The tombs belonged to the Marquis of Dai (Li Dang), his wife Lady Dai, and their son. Incredibly, a trove of more than 200 silk manuscripts were contained in the son's tomb. Seven medical manuscripts among these are considered to be the oldest medical manuscripts ever found in China.

Dunhuang Cave Manuscripts

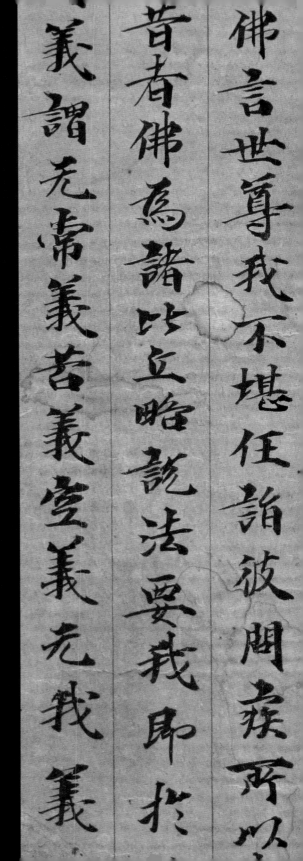

Dunhuang was a former capital of China and is located in Central Asia, to the west of Xian. In the early 1900s, 492 sealed caves were discovered there containing over 50,000 Buddhist manuscripts, including paintings, sculptures, and all sorts of written documents. This is probably the largest collection of ancient Buddhist art in the world. An inscription in the first cave in the Mogao Grottoes states that the cave was made in A.D. 366 and it contains materials dating from the fourth to the 12th centuries.

▶ A typical Tang period Buddhist Sutra fragment from Dunhuang.

2 Discovery and History of the Dead Sea Scrolls

A CHANCE DISCOVERY BY A YOUNG BEDOUIN SHEPHERD WAS TO PROVIDE THE ACADEMIC AND RELIGIOUS WORLD WITH A CORPUS OF DOCUMENTS WHOSE EXTENT HAS YET TO BE FULLY EXPLORED.

Introduction

It is amazing that some of the most significant archeological discoveries have been made by accident and by people doing normal everyday things. The story of the Dead Sea Scrolls takes place in 1947 near the northwest shore of the Dead Sea in the Holy Land, about nine miles south of Jericho and 13 miles east of Jerusalem. The Dead Sea, located between Israel and Jordan, is the lowest body of water in the world. It lies 1,300 feet below sea level and is about 50 miles long and 10 miles wide. The Dead Sea is so named because of its high salt content, which makes it uninhabitable by all but the tiniest of life forms, namely bacteria and fungi. Even these are only sparsely represented.

In this place there are numerous limestone caves in the surrounding hills. Viewing this region, you may wonder how these hills and caves were formed as they look surrealist and mysterious. Caves are formed by geological processes which involve erosion and other chemical and atmospheric processes. To understand how these caves were formed, we have to go back millions of years. At that time, this entire valley was just one large lake. Over a long period of time, the water receded and the lake dropped to lower levels. The water had by erosion produced channels in the soft

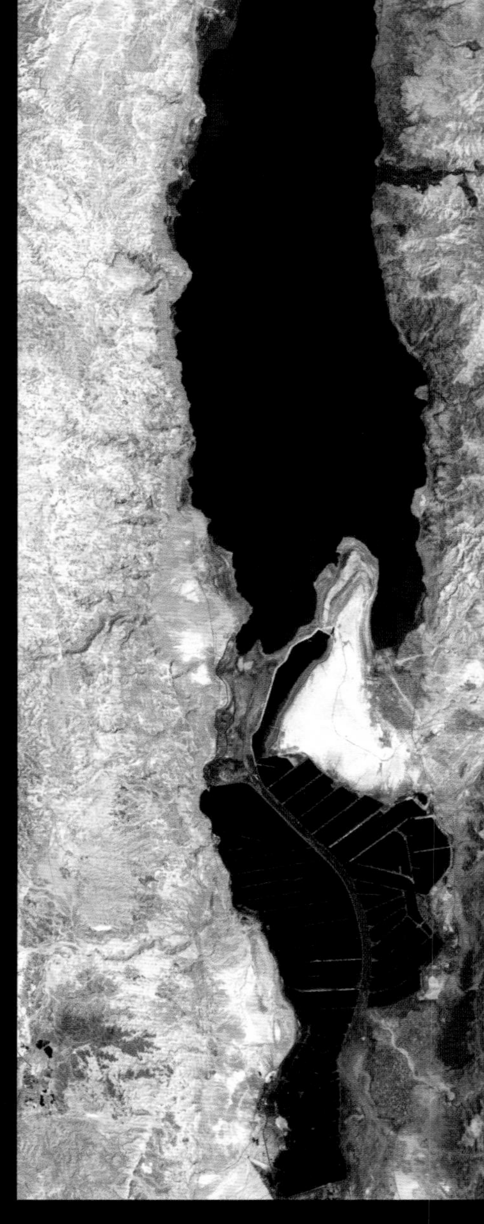

▲ An aerial view, taken by satellite, of the Dead Sea and the surrounding area.

▶ A view of the Qumran caves. The exceptionally dry climate of the area ensured that the ancient documents remained largely well preserved until their discovery after nearly 2,000 years.

rock beneath the lake and as this was exposed and dried out, it formed cavities or caves. The entrances to some of these caves were hard to see, sometimes because of where the caves were located. Others had very small openings or even openings that were covered up. These caves were perfect places for people to hide out or to conceal their treasures. Keep in mind that the ancients did not have banks in which to deposit their money or safety deposit boxes to hold their treasures. Most had to hide their valuables by burying them or concealing them in the ground or in caves like these. It is very fortunate that this area is extremely arid as this has aided the preservation of ancient manuscripts and artifacts.

There are many versions of the discovery of the Dead Sea Scrolls. We do not know for certain which ones are factual and which ones are false, and embellishment of the true facts has probably taken place. Unfortunately, all of the original discoverers of the scrolls are deceased. The most likely version of the story comes from several sources but the exact date of the discovery is questionable. It was probably in the winter of 1946–1947, between the months of November and February, since this is the time when the Bedouin tribes herd their flocks to the Dead Sea area for its greater warmth.

A Chance Discovery

The most likely version of events is as follows:

Three Bedouin cousins were grazing their goats not far from the ruins of Khirbet Qumran. Their names were Khalil Musa, Jum'a Muhammad Khalil, and Muhammad Ahmed el-Hamed, also known as Muhammad edh-Dhib, the Wolf. One of the goats disappeared from the flock and Jum'a decided to go looking for him. As he was climbing up one of the cliffs, he noticed an open cave and threw a stone into it. We do not know if he threw the stone into the cave to frighten the goat out or whether he went in there, or maybe he was simply throwing stones as a pastime while looking for the goat. It was just one of the many ordinary caves on this sea cliff. He was startled to hear an unexpected sound. Instead of the familiar sound

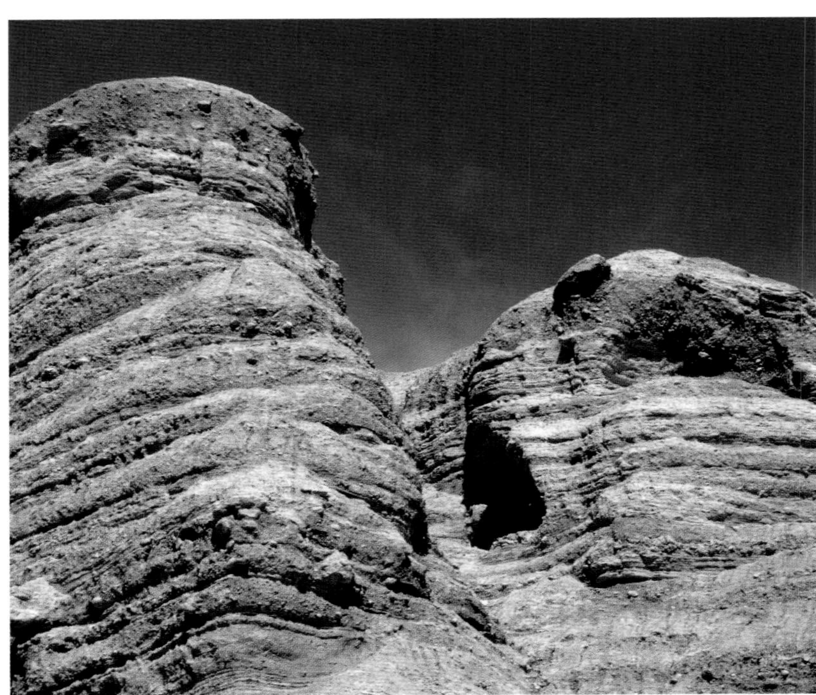

▶ In addition to the protection offered by the dry climate, the inaccessibility of the caves also served to protect the valuable documents.

of the stone falling on rocks or sand, he heard a crashing sound like the breaking of pottery. He went back to tell his two cousins and they agreed to explore the opening with him at another time, since it was getting late and they needed to get back to camp with the goats.

Either the next day or the day after that, Muhammad edh-Dhib, who was the youngest and a teenager, returned to the site by himself to explore the cave that Jum'a had discovered. Later, the other two cousins were mad at him for going back to the cave without them. When he reached the cave, he squeezed through the small cave opening. The cave dimensions were about 25 feet long, seven feet wide, and eight feet high. Inside he found ten intact pottery jars and many pottery fragments. Archeologists have determined that originally there were about 40 jars in the cave, but today we only have two intact ones. Maybe the others were broken by someone who had entered the cave before, or maybe the cousins broke them looking for treasure inside the jars. We will never know for sure, but what an unfortunate loss to archeology!

▼ A large terracotta jar of the type into which the scrolls were carefully placed for safe keeping.

The jars were about two feet high. Muhammad looked inside several of the intact jars searching for treasure and was disappointed that most were empty. Then he looked inside one of the jars and saw three ancient-looking manuscripts. Two of the manuscripts were wrapped up in a linen cloth; the other one had no wrappings. The scrolls were somewhat decayed and faded and greenish looking. They were covered with a kind of pitch or tar-like substance to protect them.

He took these scrolls back to his camp and we do not know how long they stayed there, only that they were hung on a tent pole for some length of time and that eventually the three cousins decided to try to sell them. We also know that at some time all three cousins returned to the cave to search it again.

These three scrolls were The Habakkuk Commentary, The Community Rule or Manual of Discipline, and the Great Isaiah Scroll. Jum'a and Khalil took the scrolls into Bethlehem, which was nearby, to see how much they could get for them. Nobody seemed interested in buying them so they decided to try the local cobbler or shoemaker. Some have speculated that the cousins believed the shoemaker could use them for scrap materials in his shoe repairs but I think this was unlikely. They must have known these scrolls could be valuable. The shoemaker's name was Khalil Eskander Shahin and, interestingly, he also dabbled as a dealer in antiques. That was very fortunate, as he recognized that these scrolls might be of some value. How much, he did not know, but he offered to try to find a buyer for them in return for a commission. They agreed and left the scrolls with Shahin. In the summer of 1947, Khalil, Jum'a, and a friend of Shahin went back to the cave to see whether they could find any more scrolls. By exploring and digging throughout the cave, they discovered a further four scrolls.

▼ Khalil Eskander Shahin, a shoemaker who also traded in antiques and artefacts, with whom the two Bedouin shepherds left the scrolls.

Another version of the story tells that, following the search for the goat, the next day, one of the young men went back to the cave alone and took only the stone jars, leaving the manuscripts behind. Thinking the jars were worth something, he loaded them onto his donkey. He took the jars to the town of Bethlehem and tried to sell them, but no one was interested. The story goes that he then went back the next day to fetch the manuscripts.

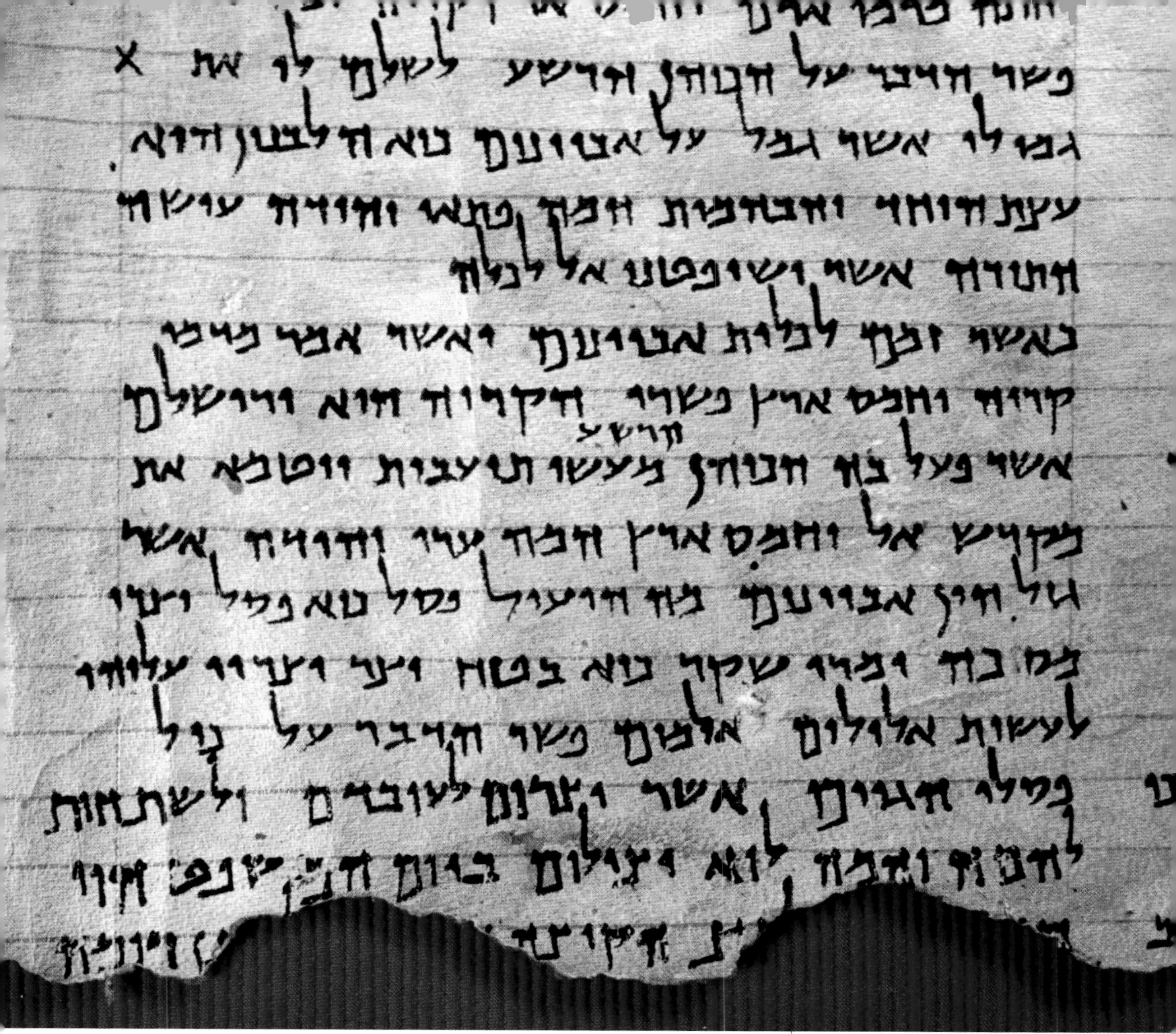

These scrolls that Shahin possessed and was trying to sell came to the attention of the Metropolitan (or Bishop) of St. Mark's Syrian Orthodox church in Jerusalem, Mar Athanasius Yeshua Samuel. Metropolitan Samuel eventually met up with Shahin and bought

▲ A section of the well preserved Habakkuk Commentary scroll, which was one of the four additional scrolls amongst the second batch of discoveries.

▲ Professor of Archeology at the Hebrew University in Jerusalem, Eleazar L. Sukenik, seen studying one of the scroll documents early in 1950.

four of the seven scrolls from him for just over $30. The cousins received $20 and Shahin kept his one third percent commission of $10. That must have been the deal of the century. Believe it or not, when Samuel was first shown the scrolls and was inspecting them, he broke off a small piece of one of the scrolls and burned it to determine if it was made of an animal hide. We know now that the four scrolls he purchased were an almost complete copy of the Isaiah Scroll, the Habakkuk Commentary, a paraphrase of parts of Genesis, and the Manual of Discipline, also called the Community Rule.

◄ Part of a scroll known as the "Trever Fragment" after John Trever, a member of the American School of Oriental Research in Jerusalem.

In the hope of selling the other three, Shahin contacted individuals at the American School of Oriental Research in Jerusalem. John Trever, a member of this institute, photographed some of these scrolls, which were later published. During this time, Eleazar L. Sukenik, a professor of archeology at the Hebrew University in Jerusalem, heard about these scrolls and offered to purchase the other three from Shahin, which he did in 1947. He recognized their significance and importance. He had purchased the War Scroll, the Thanksgiving Scroll, and an incomplete copy of Isaiah.

Thus far, few people had heard of this discovery and even fewer were aware of what a fantastic archeological find it was. It was not until April 1948, about a year after the find, that the general public became aware of the Dead Sea Scrolls. Both Sukenik and the American scholars came out with press releases, independently, at that time. Now the world would hear of these scrolls and the term Dead Sea Scrolls would become a familiar name to all mankind.

In due course, Metropolitan Samuel needed money for his church and decided to try to sell his four scrolls. He traveled to the United States with the scrolls in 1949 for the purpose of expanding his Syrian Orthodox Church in America and to cash in on his scrolls. For many years, he was not able to find a buyer. It appeared he was asking way too much for the scrolls. He wanted several million dollars for them. So, unable to sell them privately, in 1954 he placed an advertisement in the Wall Street Journal advertising his scrolls for sale. The advertisement read:

"The Four Dead Sea Scrolls" Biblical Manuscripts dating back to at least 200 B.C. are for sale. This would be an idea gift to an educational or religious institution by an individual or group.
Box F 206, The Wall Street Journal

▼ Fragments of the Dead Sea Scrolls can be seen on display at the Shrine of the Book. In spite of the special lighting, the display is changed frequently in order to preserve the documents.

By chance or destiny, Professor Sukenik's son was in the United States at the time the advertisement was placed and was told about it by a friend. It is interesting that, at around the time of the find in 1947, Sukenik offered to purchase the scrolls from Samuel but he would not sell them. Now Sukenik realized he might have a second chance. Without revealing his identity, he arranged for them to be purchased from Samuel at a price of $250,000. Thus, all seven scrolls were united again, in the possession of Professor Sukenik. He wanted them all to be returned to Israel to become part of the country's permanent collection. He believed these scrolls were important to the history of Israel and, consequently, he fulfilled his father's dream of uniting them in Israel.

The seven scrolls are currently displayed in the Shrine of the Book in Jerusalem's Israel Museum. This shrine was constructed in 1965 for the preservation and display of these scrolls. This white tiled dome structure was designed by architects Frederick Kiesler and Armand Bartos to be in the shape of the lid of one of the ancient jars that the Dead Sea Scrolls were found in.

The scrolls are encased in silk screen sheaths and the temperature and humidity is controlled to preserve them and to prevent further deterioration. The light they are exposed to is also kept to a minimum to prevent oxidation. In addition, a system of rotation has been employed so that a given scroll is only exhibited for about six months and then placed in a storeroom. Another scroll replaces this one and the rotation continues with all of the scrolls, giving each one rest from the environment. There are five authentic Dead Sea Scrolls displayed in the main hall and four in the tunnel.

▼ The Shrine of the Book Museum in Jerusalem, whose exterior design echoes the lids of the terracotta jars in which the scrolls were found.

▲ The tower of the Rockefeller Museum in Jerusalem, where additional scroll fragments are stored.

Not all of the scrolls and fragments are housed at the Shrine of the Book. Some are at the Rockefeller Museum in east Jerusalem, some fragments are at the Bibliothèque Nationale de Paris, a fragment known as the McGill fragment is in Canada, and the Department of Antiquities in Jordan houses the Copper Scroll. There are probably additional fragments in the possession of individuals who obtained them in some way or another.

A visitor to the Shrine of the Book can see, in the center of the upper floor of the shrine, the large Isaiah Scroll wrapped around a large Torah handle drum. If you think about it, wrapping an ancient scroll this way (outward) is opposite to the way it is meant to be rolled (inward). The brittle scroll would break apart if wrapped in this way. To overcome this conundrum what is actually on display is an aged Xerox copy of the Isaiah Scroll. Replicas of scroll jars and other historical reproductions can be purchased in the museum's gift shop.

When the location of the cave became known, other scholars and archeologists investigated it and found other fragments still left there. It appears that some of the fragments in this cave were pieces broken off from the scrolls which the cousins took. They must have done this by accident when removing them hastily from the jars. There were many other fragments, which were found to originate from scrolls other than the original seven. Many believed that there must be additional caves with even more manuscripts yet to be discovered, so searches were carried out by archeologists, and even the Bedouin, looking for more loot to sell. It evolved into a real Indiana Jones scenario with many racing to find additional caves that concealed more scrolls.

The Jordanian government decided that, as the Bedouins were experts at finding these scrolls, they would offer to buy any scrolls from them for $5 per square inch. This was a good offer which the Bedouins accepted and, fortunately, most of their finds were sold and did not end up on the black market. Some probably were sold underground but the number is likely to have been minimal.

▼ The central chamber of the Shrine of the Book in Jerusalem where the bulk of the Dead Sea Scrolls are to be found.

▲ Cave 11, which was the final cave to be discovered in 1956, some nine years after the first scrolls were discovered.

It was not until 1952 that a second cave was discovered that contained additional scrolls. This cave is known as Cave 2. Four more caves were discovered with scrolls and fragments over the next several years and named Caves 3, 4, 5, and 6, followed by four more named Caves 7, 8, 9, and 10. In 1956, the last cave, Cave 11, was discovered. Were there more caves with even more historical and valuable scrolls just waiting to be discovered?

In 1995, the Israel Antiquities Authority decided to mount a large exploration involving hundreds and hundreds of caves in the cliffs in this region using modern technology. A few additional artifacts of different time periods were found but nothing related to the Dead Sea Scrolls.

Controversy about Publication

One of the questions many people have raised about the Dead Sea Scrolls is why did it take so long to publish the contents of the scrolls and their translations? The first seven scrolls were found in Cave 1 in 1947. By 1955 nine more caves had been discovered and the last, Cave 11, was discovered in 1956. It was not until 1991 that all of the scrolls and fragments were made available to the public. Let us trace the history of their publication.

All the scrolls from Cave 1 were published in the 1950s. A team of eight men published the first volume in 1955. A second volume was published in 1961, and in 1962 a third volume was published, consisting of the texts from Caves 2, 3, 5, and 10. Cave 4 had the most abundant fragments, but little of this material was published until late 1982. This delay in publishing the materials from

◀ Cave 1, the first cave discovered in 1947, contained the first seven scrolls to be found, details of which were published in 1955.

Cave 4 was a major concern to most scholars. Some even thought there was a conspiracy because some of the material from Cave 4 was threatening to Christianity and even to Judaism. As there was a predominance of Catholic scholars on the team, many believed the Vatican was involved in this conspiracy. We will see that this was not true. Many suggestions have been made as to why there was a delay of over 40 years in publishing these materials. It is interesting to note that many scholars refer to this period as "the battle for the

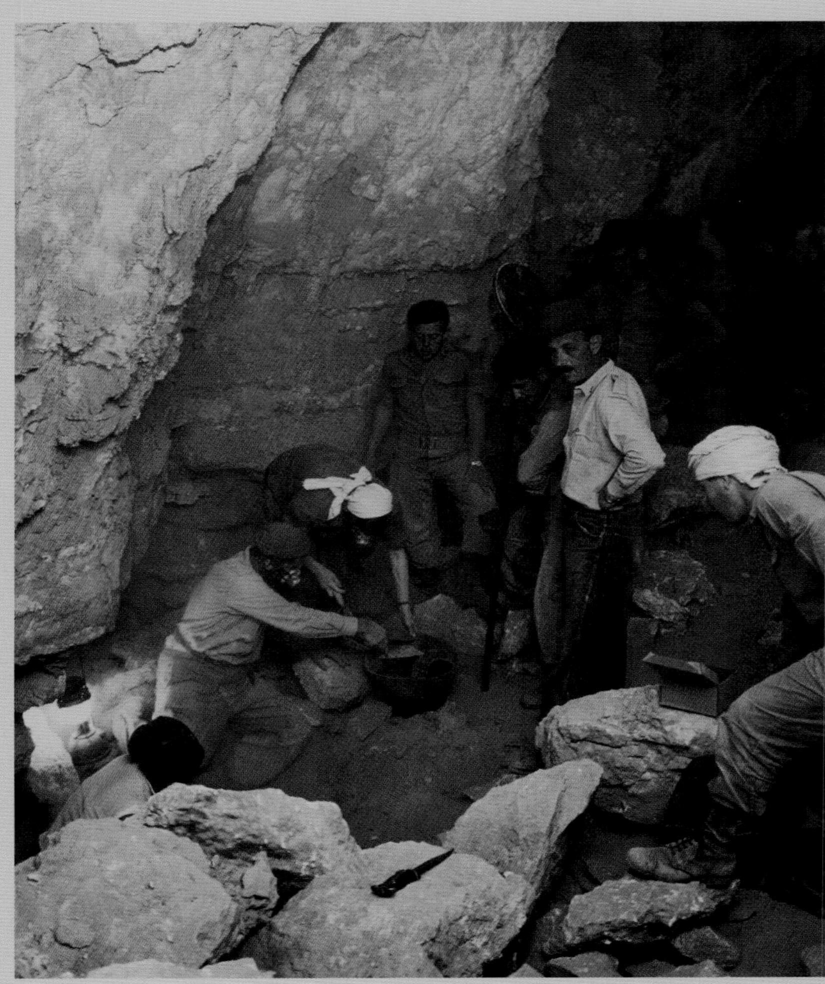

▶ World renowned Israeli archeologist Yigael Yadin, who received the Israel Prize for his thesis on the translation of the Dead Sea Scrolls, is seen here supervising excavations in Wadi Qumran in 1956.

▲ The interior of Cave 4, which contained the largest number of fragments. Because of the extensive research required, information about these was not published until 1982.

scrolls." The most logical reason for the delay is that the group of translators was far too small and that this was not a full-time job for them. Most had other jobs or university appointments and could not devote all their time to this project. It also appears that after an initial enthusiasm for the project, many lost interest and did not invest the time they should have. Some of these scholars were very possessive of the scrolls and, feeling that they were their own property, were reluctant to share them with others. Also, most scholars want to be thorough and accurate in whatever they publish or release, so they may have wanted to tie all the loose ends together before any publication or release of information was made. It should be stated that a fourth volume was published in 1965, and in 1968 and 1977 a fifth and sixth volume were published containing some of the scrolls from Cave 4.

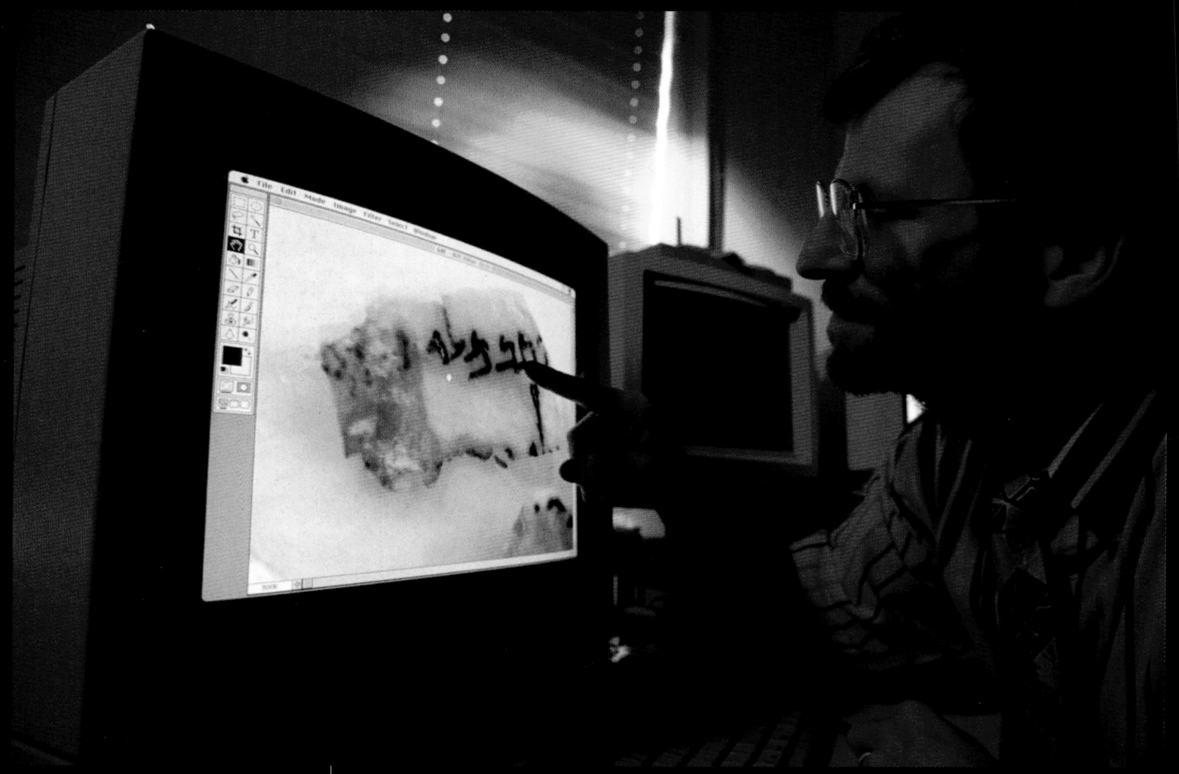

▲ Scrolls researcher Gregory Bearman is seen analyzing one of the Dead Sea Scrolls. Together with his fellow researcher Bruce Zuckerman, Bearman developed a technique which uses infrared imaging and computer software to digitally enhance the scrolls.

The first concordance is published

A major event occurred in 1991. Back in 1957, Joseph A. Fitsmyer produced a concordance of the words from the scrolls and fragments from Cave 4. He completed it in 1988 and this handwritten concordance, of which only 30 copies were made, was distributed to only a few select scholars. Each word listed in the concordance had a word on either side of it. Therefore, theoretically you could put the entire text of the scrolls together like a puzzle. Which, in fact, was exactly what Martin Abegg, a very enterprising graduate student, did using only a desktop computer to reconstruct the texts from Cave 4. Ben Zion Wacholder and Martin Abegg published the text of Cave 4 based on this concordance on September 4, 1991 and right after this, other institutions that had been given copies of the scrolls and fragments previously for safekeeping decided to make their copies available to qualified scholars. The Israel Antiquities Authority had no alternative but to announce, on October 29, 1991, that the scrolls would be now open to all researchers.

A tragic part of this story is that the Bethlehem cobbler and antiquity dealer, Shahin, decided to hide some large scroll fragments. Maybe he thought the price of the scrolls would rise and he could then sell them or maybe he wanted to prevent the antiquities department from confiscating them. We do not know the reason, but the story goes that he buried these in his backyard. Later, when he dug them up, he found that they had rotted and were destroyed. We will never know what these scroll materials could have contained.

▼ Religious scholars have also taken part in research. Here, a priest of the Ecole Biblique studies fragments of the scrolls at the Rockefeller Museum in Jerusalem.

3

Classification of the Texts

COMPRISING A TOTAL OF 60,000 FRAGMENTS FROM AN ESTIMATED 900 SEPARATE DOCUMENTS, THE SCROLLS ARE A VAST JIGSAW PUZZLE THAT IS STILL BEING ANALYZED AND CATALOGED BY SCHOLARS.

Introduction

We have learned that the Dead Sea Scrolls were discovered in 11 caves along the northwest shore of the Dead Sea, beginning from the discovery of the first cave in 1947 to the last one in 1956. The majority of the scrolls were written in Hebrew but some were written in Greek and Aramaic. Most were written on parchment (animal skins from calves, goats, or sheep) but some were written on papyrus (produced from the papyrus plant), and one on copper. The ink used to write the scrolls was carbon based. Several intact scrolls were found but the majority were isolated fragments. In fact, over 60,000 fragments were recovered from the 11 caves and many were heavily damaged. Experts have identified almost 900 separate texts of varying length, for some of which only one fragment survives. Like ancient Hebrew, they were written from right to left without any punctuation. Without the benefit of punctuation, separating the text into words, sentences, and paragraphs has been the work of researchers.

Seven intact manuscripts were found in Cave 1. Cave 11 is the only other cave that contained intact manuscripts, the remaining caves containing mostly scroll fragments. The largest number of fragments was found in Cave 4, which contained over 15,000.

◄ Cave 4 was found to contain more than 15,000 scroll fragments.

► Scrolls of leather parchment of the sort found in the caves and which have proved to be so durable.

The Bible Canon

The Dead Sea Scrolls contain both texts that are in our currently accepted Bible and also texts that are biblical in nature but were never included in the Bible. This is fascinating, since these texts could supplement and fill in gaps in modern day Bibles. Firstly, one needs to examine how the Bible was formed.

▲ An early 15th century illustration of scenes from the Book of Genesis which, together with the other books of the Old Testament, originally came from an oral tradition.

Many people think that the Bible has a fixed number of books from Genesis to Revelation, and that this is how it has always been, but this is not true. The accepted canon or official list of books of the Bible has not always been the same and in fact today, Jews, Protestants, Catholics, and orthodox Greeks each claim different numbers of books for their canon or sacred scripture. To understand this, let us travel back in time. As the books of the Bible were being written down from oral tradition and eventually completed, some scribe or editor started putting together groups of books or writings that he felt were important to his religious community. At first, different groups may have chosen different materials for their sacred scriptures, so there was not a set number of books. Now most Bible scholars believe that composition of most of the books of the Old Testament began from about the sixth century B.C., and that the books were in common circulation by about 300 B.C. It was not until about A.D. 100 that a decision was made as to which books should be included in the list of accepted sacred scripture and which should not. Around the eighth century A.D., a collection of Hebrew scriptures was put together by a group of scribes known as the Masoretes. This Bible is called the Masoretic Text. Another version of the Old

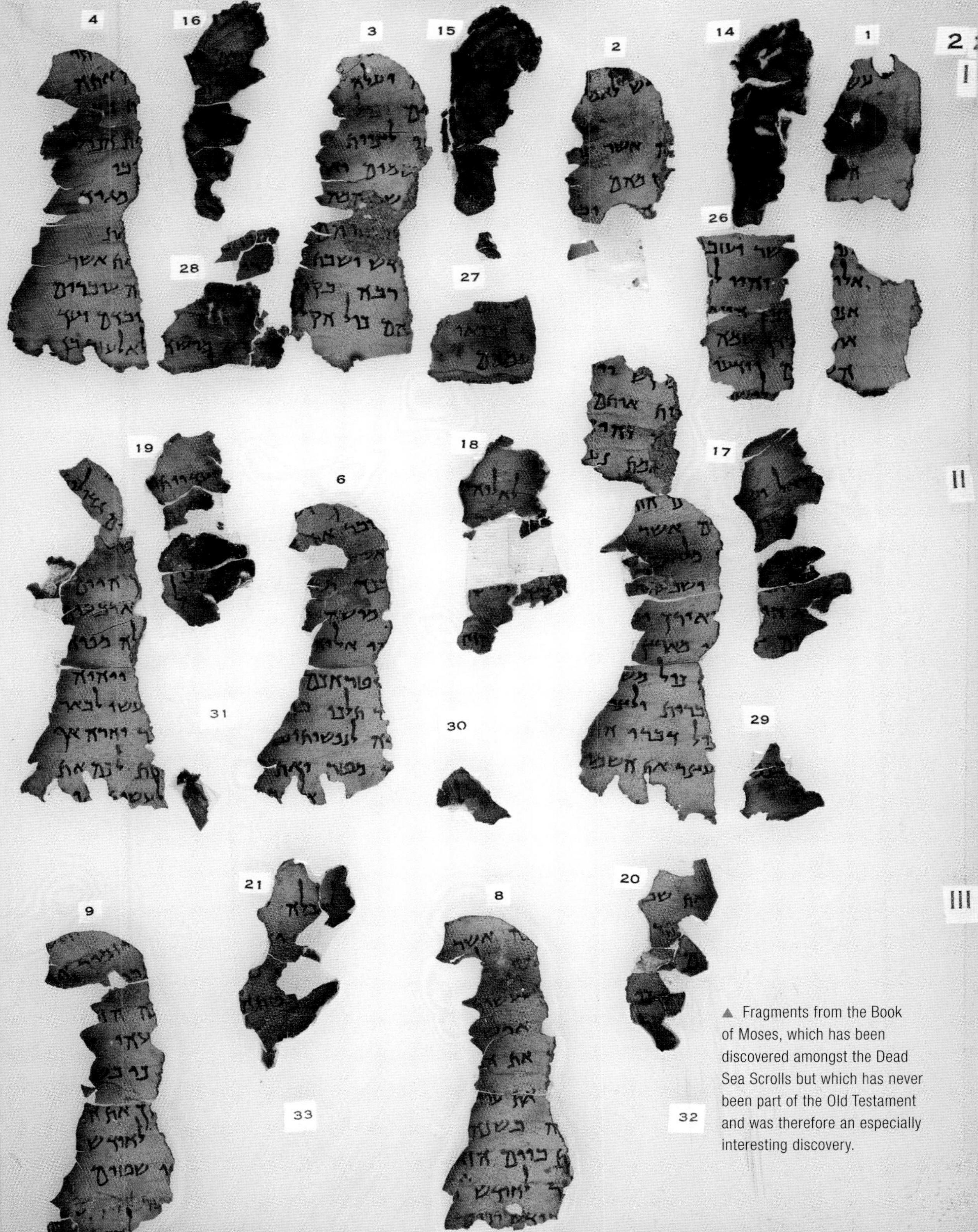

▲ Fragments from the Book of Moses, which has been discovered amongst the Dead Sea Scrolls but which has never been part of the Old Testament and was therefore an especially interesting discovery.

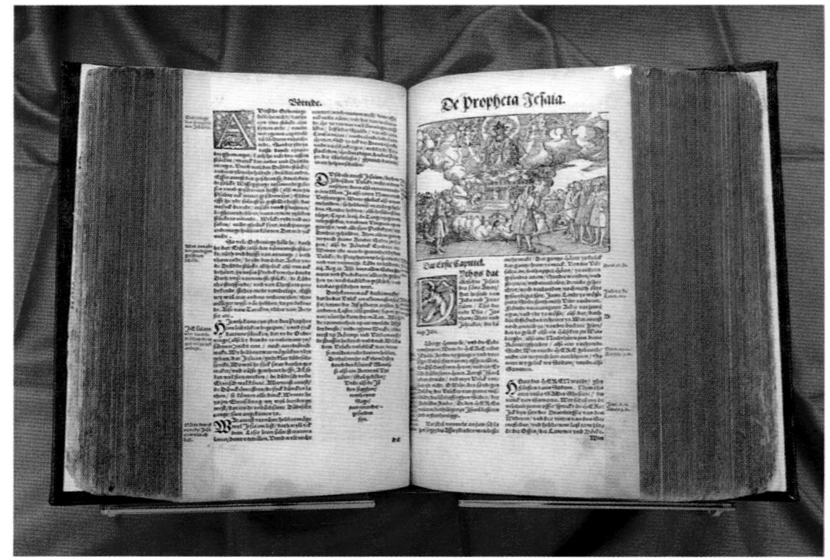

▶ Martin Luther's translation of the Bible, first published in 1534, gained instant popularity largely because of the accessibility of its language. It remains in print to this day.

Testament was put together in the first century A.D. in Greek. This Bible was for the Greek-speaking world, while the Masoretic Text was the Bible for the Hebrew-speaking world.

Not all of the known books of scriptures at that time were accepted as authoritative scriptures and were included; many were left out. In fact, the Roman Catholic Bible has additions in its Old Testament (seven additional books and additional material to other books), which the Protestant Bible does not. Also, the Greek Orthodox version has four additional books and a psalm not contained in the Roman Catholic Bible. Each religious group decided which books they believed were the official books for their sacred scripture and these books comprised their canon. The important point is that the number of books was not fixed until a certain time and many books considered to be scripture were not included in the Bible. Some of these books missing from the Bible were not passed down and so, up until the time of the discovery of the Dead Sea Scrolls, we had no idea of the existence of some of these texts.

Canons of the Roman Catholic, Protestant, and Greek Orthodox Churches

The Protestant Bible consists of 39 books. Modern translations include the King James Version (KJV), New International Version (NIV), and the Revised Standard Version (RSV).

The Roman Catholic Bible contains these 39 books and seven additional books, yielding a total of 46 books. Versions of the Roman Catholic Bible include the New American Standard, the Jerusalem Bible, and the Douay Rheims Bible. The seven extra books are Judith, The Wisdom of Solomon, Tobit, Sirach or Ecclesiasticus, Baruch with the letter of Jeremiah, and First and Second Maccabees. Supplementary material to the books of Esther and Daniel also distinguish the Roman Catholic Bible from the Protestant version. Additions to Daniel include The Prayer of Azariah and the Song of the Three Young Men (added after Dan. 3:23 and Susanna, and Bel and the Dragon.)

In addition to all the above books, the Greek Orthodox Bible includes the two books of Esdras, the third and fourth books of Maccabees, and Psalm 151.

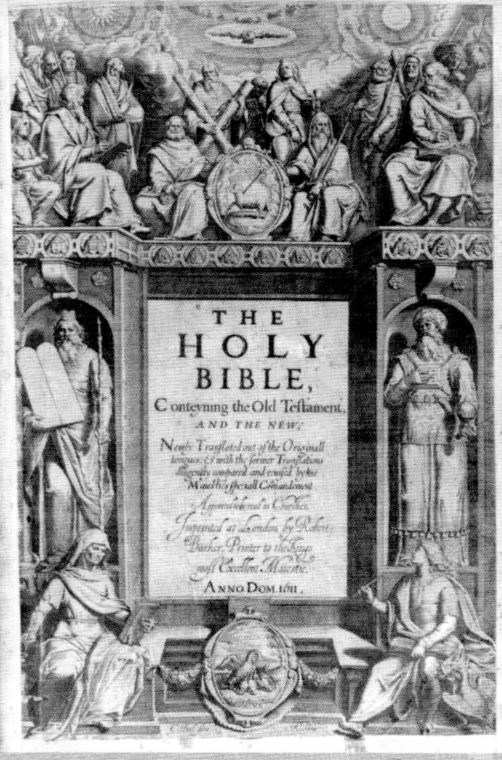

▼ The frontispiece to the English King James Version first published in 1611 which excludes the seven additional books of the Roman Catholic Bible.

How Texts from the Dead Sea Scrolls are Classified

Several different methods or classification systems have been used to put the scroll texts into categories, depending on their content.

Hartmut Stegemann, a scroll researcher from Germany who first put forth his method in the 1990s, proposed one of the best classification systems. He classifies the scrolls into four major categories: Biblical, Sectarian, Nonsectarian, and Unidentified Texts. The table below shows the relative percentages and numbers of scrolls in each category. For simplicity and memory, you can approximate the numbers as Biblical a third, Sectarian a third, and Nonsectarian and Unidentified a third. In the last group, there are about twice as many Nonsectarian texts as Unidentified.

▼ Scroll scholar Yigael Yadin was influential in his work on a number of the key scrolls, including the Genesis Apocryphon, the War Scroll and the Temple Scroll.

Biblical	223 texts	29%
Nonsectarian	192 texts	25%
Sectarian	249 texts	33%
Unidentified	96 texts	13%

Using his classification system, let us explore some examples in each category.

The Biblical Scrolls

The biblical scrolls and fragments that have been found in the caves contain at least some part of every book of the Old Testament, except Esther. This is significant since these scrolls and fragments are thousands of years older than any manuscripts or fragments we of Bible text before 1947. The oldest known Bible manuscript fragment before this was from about the tenth century A.D.

To have these books of the Bible that go back 2,000 years is important since, from these books, we can tell whether and how much the Bible has changed during centuries of being copied, edited, and passed down. We can usually judge the importance of a text to the community by the number of copies they may have had. The book of Isaiah is one of the most represented books in the Dead Sea Scrolls collection and, in fact, 19 copies have been identified. Another book represented in great numbers is the Psalms, of which 39 copies have been found. The Psalms were very important to the community since they must have used them in their liturgy and for personal prayers. Twenty copies of the book of Deuteronomy have also been found. These scrolls, the oldest Old Testament manuscripts ever found, are 1,000 years older than anything we had before.

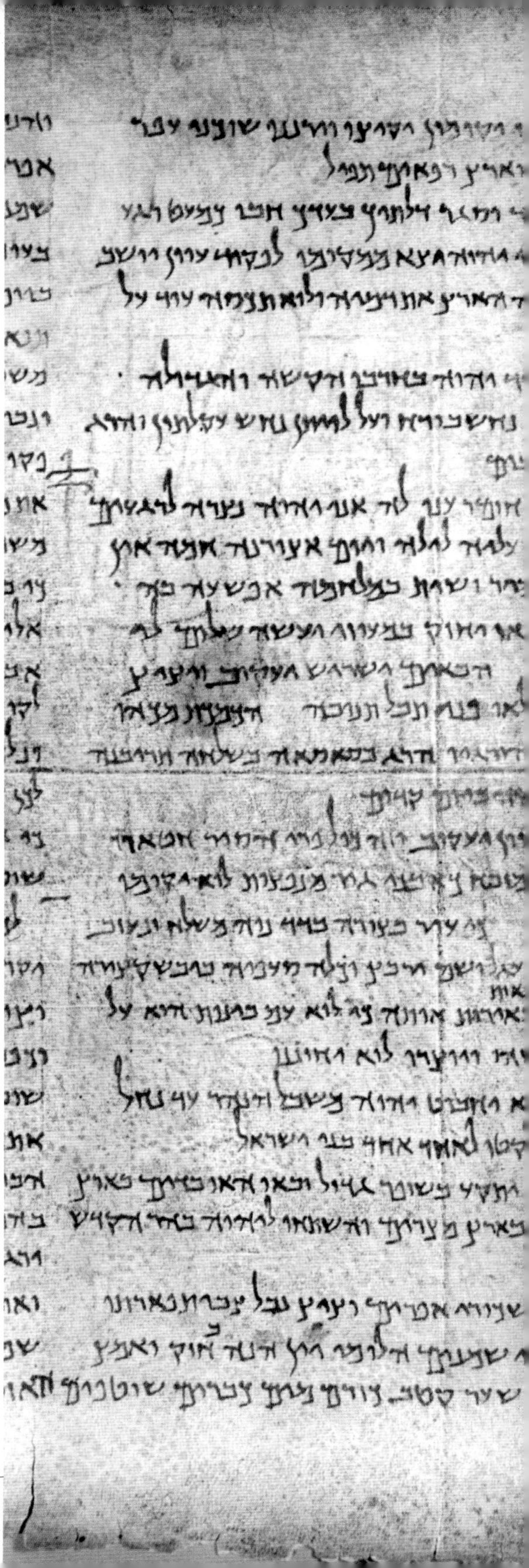

▶ The Dead Sea Scrolls are as much as 1,000 years older than any Old Testament manuscripts previously available.

What is extremely interesting about some of the biblical sections of the Dead Sea Scrolls is that there are writings not found in our current Bibles. Many are attributed to well-known Bible personages, such as Moses and Joseph. There are also unknown prophecies in the Dead Sea Scrolls that claim to be attributed to the prophets Daniel, Jeremiah, and Ezekiel. There are words of Joseph, Judah, and others that we do not find in our current Bible and also unknown psalms also attributed to King David. How exciting it is to be able to read this material that was left out of the Bibles.

▼ Previously unknown prophecies contained in the Dead Sea Scrolls have been attributed, amongst others, to Jeremiah, depicted here in a painting by Rembrandt.

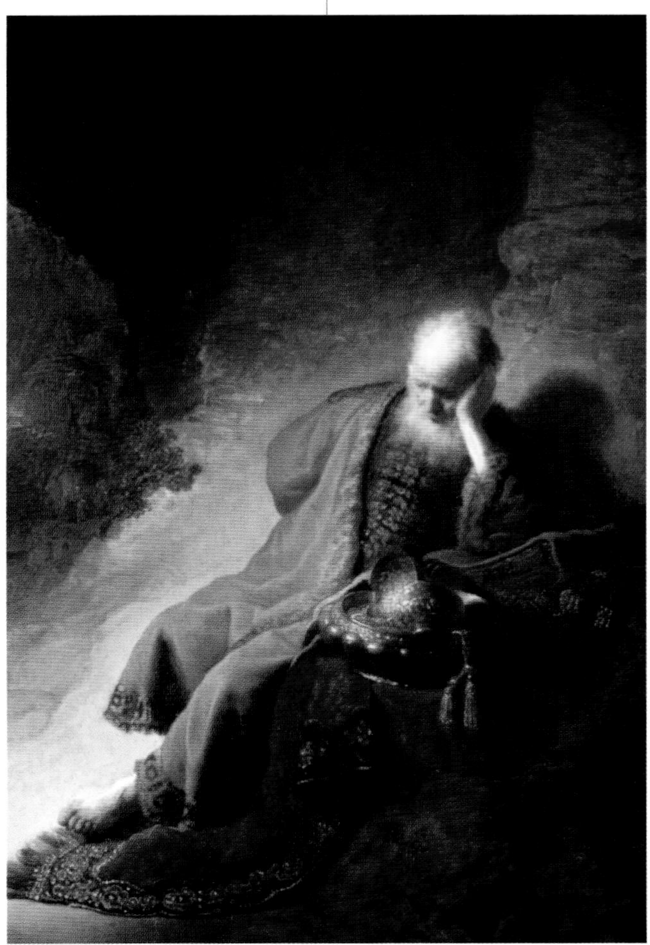

It is important to emphasize that not all the texts in the Dead Sea Scrolls that we also have in our Bibles are exactly the same. Some of the books in our modern Bibles differ from those of the Dead Sea Scrolls in a significant manner, whereas others are almost very similar. The Isaiah Scroll is more or less identical to the book of Isaiah in our current Bibles. There are other books with slight differences. Two versions of the book of Jeremiah were found; one is very similar to our biblical Jeremiah, but the other is different in length and order. It is about 15 percent shorter than our modern version and the order of events in the book is different. Many of the psalms are also different, especially Psalms 90 to 150, which are also in our modern Bibles. In addition, they are arranged in a different order. We will look are some of these differences and additions in later chapters.

▲ The Temple Scroll, one of the most important nonsectarian texts found in Qumran.

Nonsectarian Scrolls

The Temple Scroll is an example of a nonsectarian text. Two copies of this scroll were found. This text is not about the community, and is thus a nonsectarian text, but it appears to be a supplement to the Pentateuch, the first five books of the Bible. It is mainly concerned with the temple, its construction, and ritual sacrifices.

Other nonsectarian texts discuss which type of calendar to use for liturgical purposes. This was important, since the type of calendar used would determine the dates of religious festivals such as Passover, Hanukkah, etc. The two major calendars in use were the solar and lunar calendars. The lunar calendar was used by the Jewish priests at that time. The sectarian community who wrote the scrolls favored the solar calendar and believed the use of the lunar calendar was evil.

▲ One of the most fascinating nonsectarian texts is the Angelic Liturgy, which is a collection of hymns and prayers offered up to God by the angels.

The solar calendar depended on the sun's cycle whereas the lunar calendar depended on the cycle of the moon. There was, of course, a difference in the number of days, and therefore the dates of the religious festivals differed depending on which calendar was used. The lunar calendar was shorter than the solar by about ten days, and the texts clearly indicate that the group who wrote the Dead Sea Scrolls followed a solar calendar rather than a lunar one. They condemned others who chose to use a lunar calendar.

One of the most interesting nonsectarian texts relates to angels. This text, known as the Angelic Liturgy, is a collection of hymns and prayers which the angels offer up to God. It is possible that these prayers were also used to pray to the angels but they were mainly angelic prayers to God. One of the main focuses or topics of these prayers is the temple in heaven. They believed that the temple on earth was a reflection of the temple in heaven. The Rosicrucians have a saying "as above, so below." Actually, this goes back even further to ancient times when it was believed that everything happening on earth was a reflection of what was occurring in the heavens.

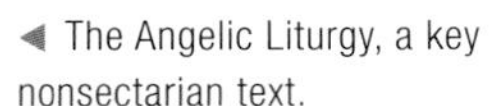

◀ The Angelic Liturgy, a key nonsectarian text.

The Sectarian Scrolls

▲ The Rule of the Community, which offers a fascinating insight into the Essene community who lived in Qumran and who compiled the Dead Sea Scrolls.

These scrolls are very important for understanding the beliefs, practices, and rituals of the community who compiled the scrolls. It also discusses the laws, rules, and regulations which they were required to follow.

The most important of the sectarian scrolls and fragments discovered is the one from Cave 1 called "Rule of the Community." This text is comprised of several parts or sections. Some think that originally there were three separate texts and that, at some time in its history, they were joined together into one scroll.

The preface or beginning of this scroll describes the goals or purposes of the community. It is a mission statement for the community, to give its members guidance to a way of life that would be pleasing in the eyes of God. They would also be protected from the end times when the wrath of God would come. It goes into details about new membership, vows, renewing vows, feast days, etc. It also talks about

▲ Astrology and divination, although rejected by Christianity, occur in many religions and appear to have been practiced in the Qumran community.

invoking blessings from God upon the members known as the Sons of Light. Curses were recited on the evil ones, the Sons of Darkness.

After this preface comes a very interesting section called the "Teaching on the Two Spirits," which tells how man is composed of both good and evil forces. The amount of good and evil in the world was held to be equal or balanced. This is similar to yin and yang and other dualistic teachings of some ancient religions. According to this text, an individual did not have a choice in how he was made, that is, how much good or evil he was created with. This was determined by God before the person was born and could not be changed or modified, so someone born with mostly evil within him would always be evil. But someone born with mostly good traits could actually become evil if he abused the good gifts given him by God.

The text quantifies the good and evil parts of which a person could be composed. Each person had a total of nine parts. Some were good and some were evil. The highest level of good a person could be born with was eight parts of good and one part of evil. The worst makeup a person could be born with was eight parts evil and one part good. There were other combinations that a person might have. It was almost like a genetic trait, being born good or evil. It was important for the community to be able to determine this in an individual since they would not want to admit a member that was predominantly made up of evil parts. They practiced astrology and certain divination techniques in order to be able to determine the amount of good and evil in an individual. They also had a belief in physiognomy, in which the physical appearance determined inner traits and characteristics, and all these techniques helped them evaluate a person.

Following this is a section called the "Manual of Discipline." As the name implies it is a text of disciplinary procedures. It describes the practices that apply specifically to members of the community. The community was led by a Master and under him were the priests, called the Sons of Zadok. This section discusses many themes, including why the community was formed, how to join, rules and regulations, and also what the specific penalties were for violating any of the rules or accepted conduct in the community. There were different degrees of penalty for different violations. These could be as minor as decreasing the amount of food a member was given at each meal or as major as being expelled from the community.

▼ The Manual of Discipline is a text that covers disciplinary practices within the Essene community.

Finally, there was a section known as the "Congregational Rule." This section contained the rules to follow when the expected Messiah appeared. Because of its theme, it is sometimes referred to as the "Messianic Rule." The idea was that the community should be prepared militarily for the end times. After this section there are blessings which are most likely to have been used in community services and gatherings.

▲ The War Scroll addresses the battle between good and evil and the eventual war that would take place in the last six years of the end times.

Another sectarian scroll, the "Damascus Document," is especially interesting. Beginning with a short history of Israel, it continues with further exhortations to people remain true to their calling, so that they will be rewarded in the end times. It also contains a section on a miscellaneous group of rules, including Sabbath observance and rules, vows, legal aspects, etc. One section deals with rules for women and children, which would have applied to the section of the community that was not the ascetic, celibate community of men.

The "War Scroll," which was found in Cave 1, is also important, as it discusses the battle between good and evil in the end times or last days. The question is whether this is a real practical manual for war or a symbolic text. Remember, they believed there was a counterpart for everything in the heavens. As with the expression "as above, so below," as the battle rages on the earth between good and evil, that is, the Sons of Light versus the Sons of Darkness, a similar battle rages in the heavens between the good and bad angels.

What did they believe this war would lead to and who would win?

They believed that this war would take place in the last six years of the end times and, obviously, that the good would win. Jerusalem would be retaken and the proper worship in the temple restored. There would be an additional 33 years of war until the destruction of all the other rebellious nations was complete.

It is interesting to note that the Cathars, a sect founded in the eleventh century in Eastern Europe, also believed in a dualistic universe. They believed that there were two divine principles that coexisted, one good and one evil. These forces had been in constant battle since the beginning of time and would continue their struggles to the end of time. All matter had been created by Satan and was considered evil, but the soul, created by God, was good and was trapped in this evil body. Thus, the struggle between body and soul, evil and good would rage on until the soul could be liberated from the body by undergoing certain practices such as fasting, prayers, and very specific ceremonies which only the Cathars could perform. This was the goal of all individuals; to attain salvation by the liberation of the soul from the body. The church persecuted the Cathars in the 13th century and they disappeared completely by the 15th century.

▲ The Cathars were dualists who saw the forces of good in constant battle with the forces of evil. Here they are seen being persecuted by Dominican monks.

Unidentified Scrolls

The final category in this classification system is unidentified texts, of which there are about 96. Experts are still working on deciphering these.

4 Working with and Dating the Scrolls

UTILIZING THE LATEST SCIENTIFIC TECHNIQUES, AND BY THE PAINSTAKING EFFORTS OF SCHOLARS FROM MANY COUNTRIES, IT HAS BEEN POSSIBLE TO DATE THE MAJORITY OF THE DOCUMENTS, ALTHOUGH THE DEBATE CONTINUES.

Introduction

Tens of thousands of scroll fragments have been found in the 11 caves of the Dead Sea region near Qumran. How does one put this massive jigsaw puzzle together to form the original 800 or more different manuscripts from which these fragments came? The experts first try to match the small fragments to form sentences, then paragraphs, then pages, and finally the completed scroll. When you buy a jigsaw puzzle, you have all the pieces, hopefully, and the picture of what the completed puzzle will look like is on the box. So you know what the final end product will be and you have all the pieces. In the case of the Dead Sea Scrolls, in many instances you do not know what the final picture will look like and most likely you do not have all the pieces, so this can be more challenging then you can imagine. Also, you do not have just one jigsaw puzzle but over 800 that you are trying to assemble at the same time. You could see it is as attempting simultaneously to assemble 800 puzzles with over 90 percent of the pieces missing.

▶ One of the scrolls from Cave 1, known as IQ Mysteries, is laid out with fragments in position, thus demonstrating the painstaking work that is required to make sense of all of the parts and fragments.

◀ Professor Bieberharant performs an intricate and delicate operation in the process of restoring a scroll in the House of the Book in 1955.

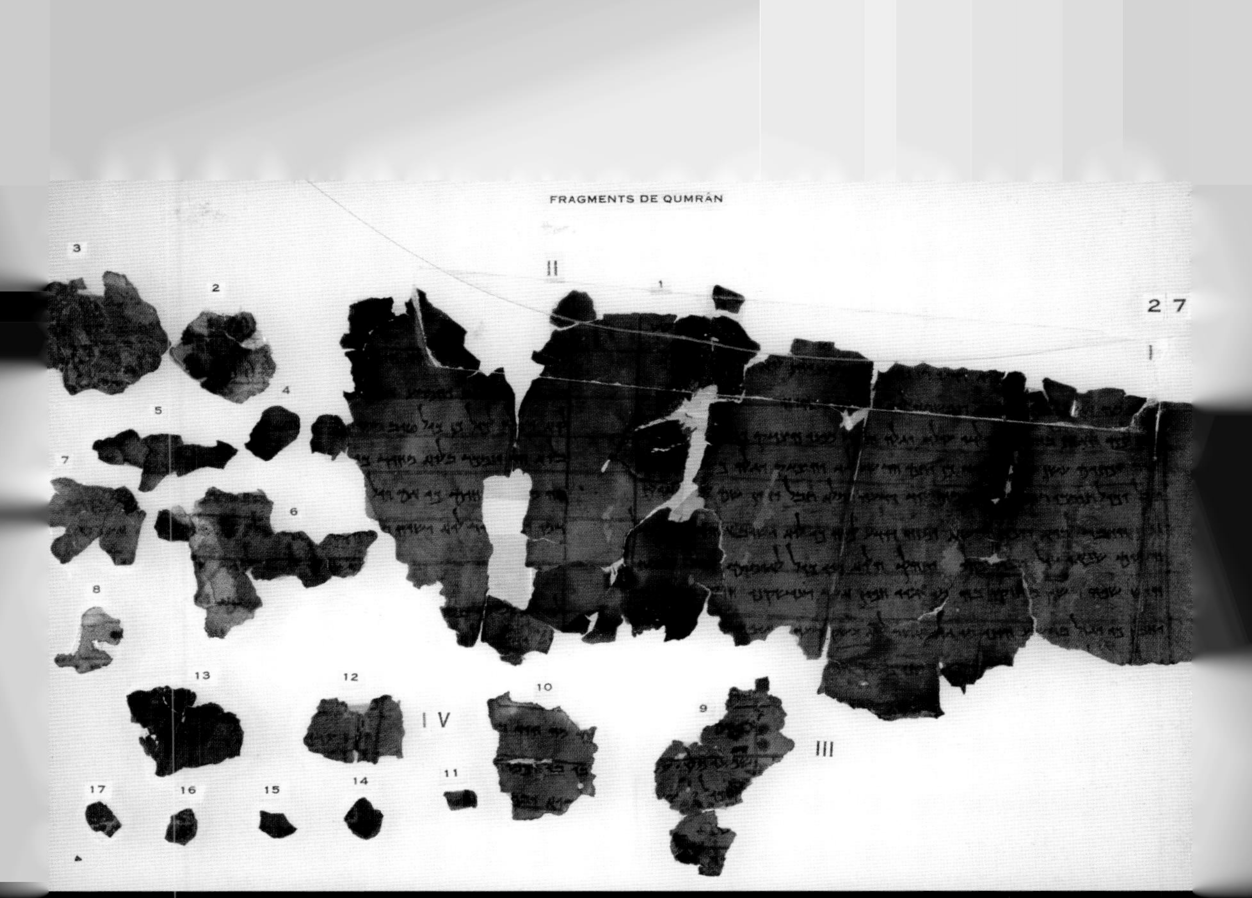

Assembling biblical texts or texts that we are familiar with is not as difficult as assembling unknown texts, since the Bible or known text serves as the picture on the box. Though it may not be the exact text, as there may be some variations, on the whole we have a good idea of how the text will read. About 20 percent of the Dead Sea Scroll documents are biblical. Another 20 percent of the documents are non biblical texts that we knew of before the discovery of the Dead Sea Scrolls. That leaves us with approximately 60 percent of the texts, which were unknown before the discovery of the Dead Sea Scrolls, so we have no way of knowing what these will say until they have been assembled. This is like assembling a jigsaw puzzle with missing pieces, with duplicate pieces, and with badly damaged pieces that are difficult to make out and without any pictures to go by. Therefore other clues are needed to help assemble these puzzles. How do the scroll researchers go about putting the scroll fragments together?

Deciphering the clues

The first step is to place the fragments on tables under glass for easy viewing. They then look for clues that might indicate an association of some fragments. Most of the fragments are composed of parchment, and a few of papyrus. Parchment is animal skin and the skins of different species of animals have different characteristics. Some fragments may have come from the skins of goats, calves, sheep, or some other animal and this parchment would be distinctive for each species of animal. The skin of individual animals within the same species would also vary, just as it does from one person to another. The skin may vary in color, thickness, and smoothness.

▼ When comparing the various fragments of a text, researchers look first for common styles of writing which will link these to the largest parts in their possession.

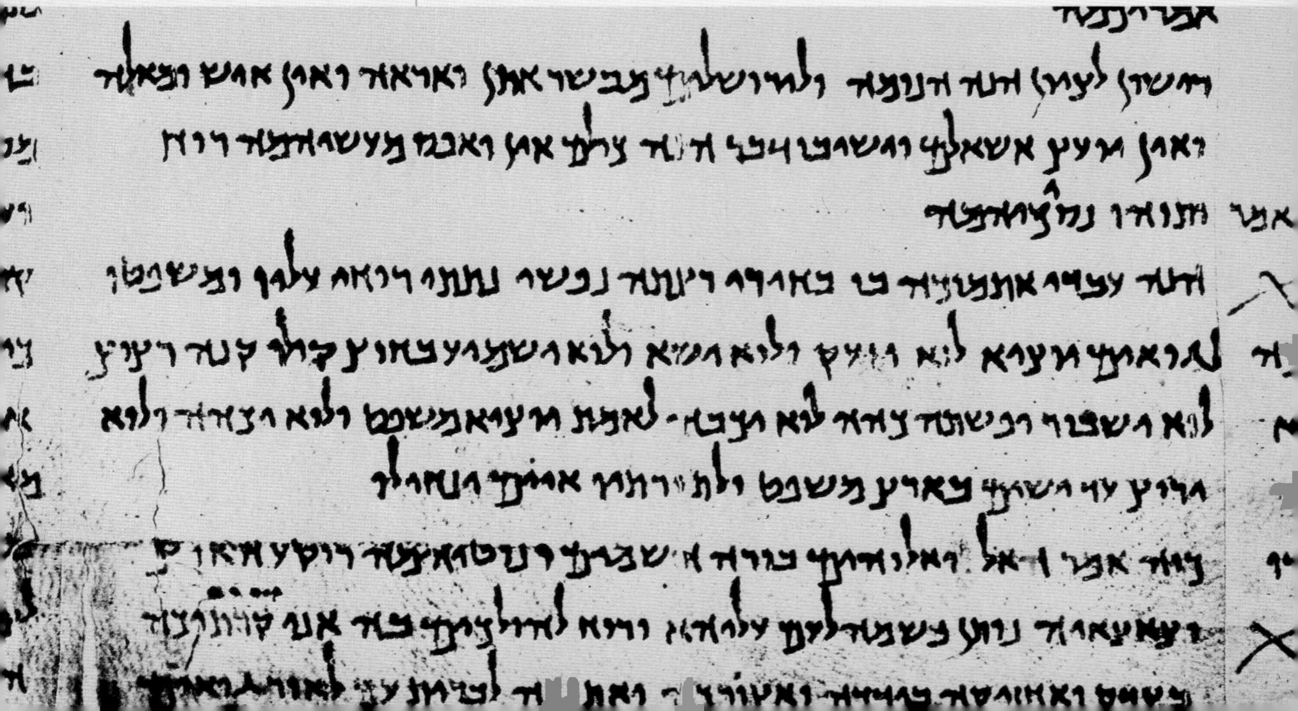

Another clue to be used is the type and style of handwriting. Fortunately, most of the scrolls were written by different scribes. Therefore, for most of the scrolls, the handwriting is unique and the fact that very few books were written down by the same scribe is providence. The experts try to match fragments by the style and form

of the handwriting. This is not an easy task as many of the fragments are badly damaged and very small, some as small as a fingernail. One clue would be any conspicuous idiosyncrasies of the handwriting of the scribe.

▲ On some scrolls, the guide lines for writers are still visible and are helpful in matching and placing the various fragments.

Another clue to use is the lines that the scribe scored on the parchment. Just like the notebook paper we used at school that has lines running horizontally to help us write the letters in a straight line, the scribes made very faint lines to help guide their characters. These lines have spacing characteristics. In addition, the number of lines per page may vary with each scribe and text, so this is another clue for identifying fragments. They can also look at how the letters are placed on the lines, either above, below, or in the middle as this would be another personal characteristic of the particular scribe writing the text.

One of the most ingenious clues that has been used turns the damage done to the scrolls to advantage. Most of the damage was caused by climate and insects. The scrolls were rolled as opposed to being flat like a sheet of paper. So, if an insect ate right through the scroll, it would leave a pattern of holes which could be used to try to fit the pieces together. Also, if a scroll was laid on its end and that got damaged due to moisture, etc. the damage could enable the end pieces to be matched up.

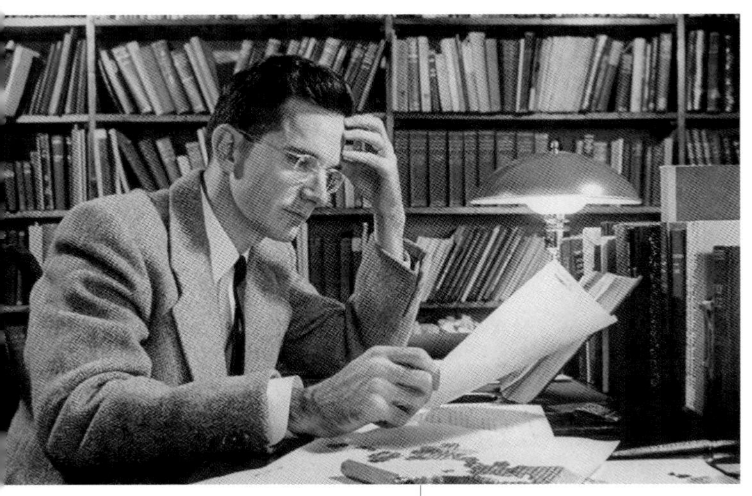

▲ Methods of study have advanced considerably over the years. Frank Cross, one of the early scholars seen here, had to make do with little more than a magnifying glass.

Just as radiocarbon dating (also known as C14 dating) revolutionized the dating process for archeological finds and manuscripts, modern technology has revolutionized the ability to identify similar fragments from the same animal. DNA testing is used to identify the animal from which each fragment came since each animal has its own, unique DNA.

It may be thought that it would be better to work with the original fragments than a photographic copy, but this is not correct. Over time, the ink fades and may be hard to read. If you photograph the fragments in infrared light, faded areas stand out distinctly and you can read the letters that were not visible or unclear. Computer technology also plays a big part in deciphering the lettering on the scrolls. The researchers have computer analysis and all kinds of computer enhancements, magnification, and digital imaging to help them. In fact, all kinds of digital and imaging software have been used in helping to decipher the faded characters and reduce the background noise, so the characters could stand out better. Even a technique called Multispectral Imaging (MSI) was used to render invisible script visible.

Once several of the fragments have been matched up and a section of the scroll can be read, the next step is to write down what these letters are on a piece of paper. The scholar will read the scroll and write down, in standard Hebrew characters, the letters he can make out on the scroll. (Areas that cannot be made out or are missing are indicated with brackets.) This process of transcribing the original written letters on the scroll to a piece of paper using standard Hebrew characters that could clearly be understood and recognized by anyone trained to read Hebrew is called the "transcription process." An analogy would be if you took notes by hand in one of your classes during the day and then typed up your notes at night, transcribing them into clear typewritten letters. The next step is to translate the Hebrew into other languages, for example, English. This is called the "translating process."

Under the system of labeling each fragment to identify where it came from, the fragments are identified by the cave they came from and given a number relating them the manuscript of which they are a part. For example, 1Q18 means that this manuscript came from Cave 1 at Qumran (Q = Qumran). Fragment 4Q276 came from Cave 4. The number after the Q represents the manuscript number. In our first example, the number 18 means that it is the 18th manuscript from Cave 1. In the second example, 276 is the 276th manuscript from Cave 4. Thus, we have a system to identify the fragments by the caves and by the manuscripts.

▶ (following spread) Here scroll researcher Gregory Bearman compares a digitally enhanced version with the original, clearly demonstrating the increased legibility even to the naked eye.

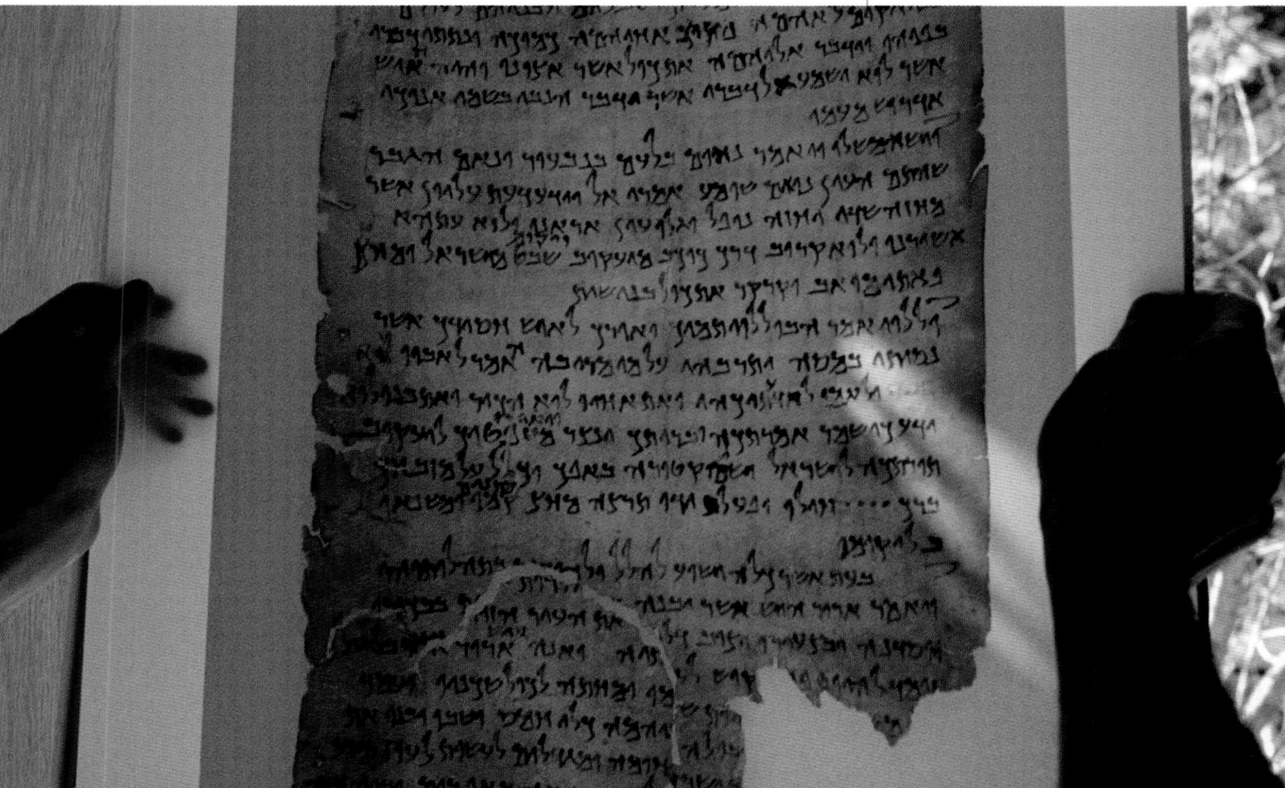

▼ Present day researchers are able to use computer technology to digitally enhance the scrolls, making previously illegible texts more accessible.

▲ During the early days of scroll research, material was not treated with as much care and attention as today, often being exposed to direct sunlight, and even cigarette ash.

The lines are numbered from the top of the column to the bottom. Damaged or missing areas are indicated by square brackets [ ]. Words reconstructed are included in these brackets, so even if there is missing text, the editor may be able to guess what was in that section, based on other scrolls and the content of the materials.

A word must be said about the history of the conservation of the scrolls. It appears that the early team did not really treat the scrolls the way they should have from a conservationist point of view. Some of the researchers used masking tape to tape fragments together. Also, the fragments were left on the table exposed to the sun for long periods of time, windows were left open, and one researcher even applied clove oil to some of the fragments to help bring out the script, which was fairly legible. The environment was not satisfactory to say the least, and the way in which the scrolls were treated is really a disgrace.

It is hard to believe that these scholars did not know better. It was even said that some smoked cigarettes around the scrolls and that ashes may have been dropped onto them. No one made a record of the original condition of the fragments.

It should be mentioned that one of the caves contained a small inscription on a piece of pottery. This type of artifact is called an ostracon. The room in which the fragments were assembled was called the scrollery.

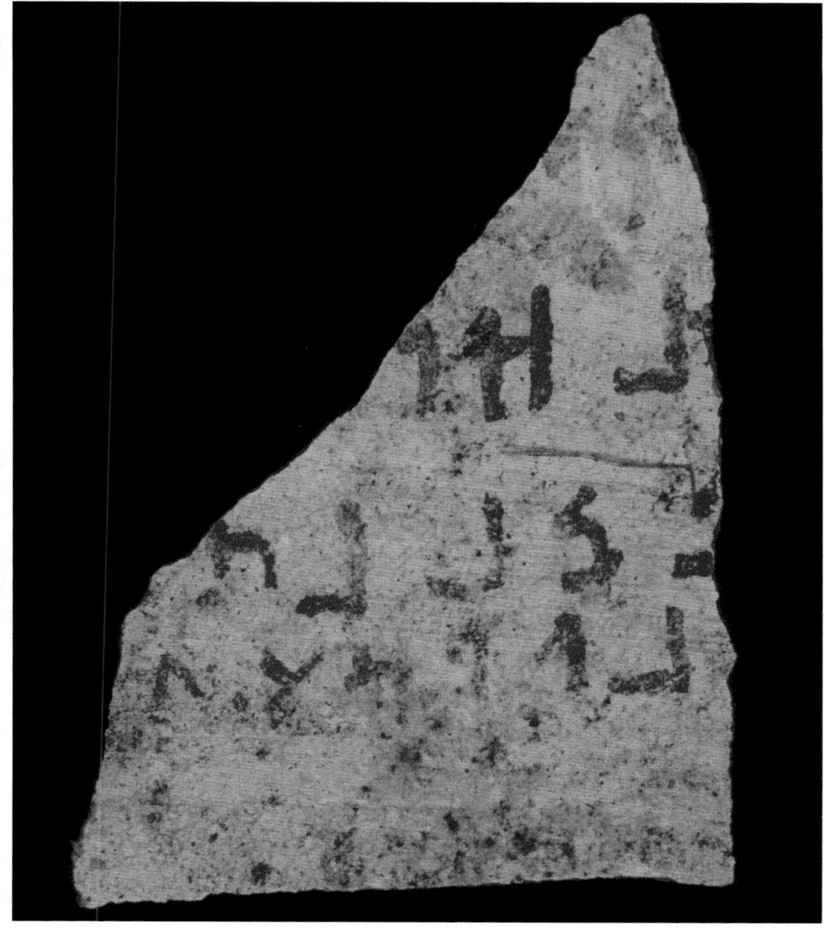

◀ Researchers have returned to the caves, retrieving everything which might prove useful in analyzing and decoding the scrolls, such as the small piece of pottery with writing on it, shown here.

Dating Ancient Manuscripts

Before the advent of radiocarbon dating, ancient manuscripts were sometimes dated based on the type of script that was used. As written languages evolved, so did the script. Often it is possible to come up with a range of dates in which a certain type and style of script was used. This was not always accurate, but sometimes it was the only information the experts had to work with. For example, in the evolution of the English language, black letter script was used from about the 12th to the 16th centuries. Most Bibles produced during this period had this type of script, so if you found a Bible that was not a reproduction and was in black letter, you would know it was printed during this time. Therefore each language, including Hebrew, had its own evolution of style, characters, and script.

▼ The date of this 14th century Psalter can be fairly accurately identified because of its use of black letter text.

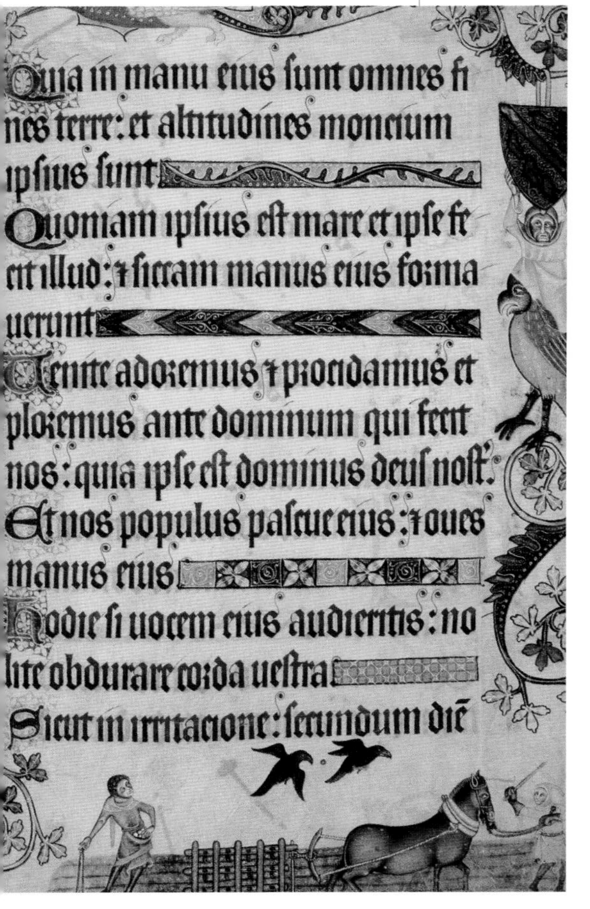

Quia in manu eius sunt omnes fi
nes terre: et altitudines montium
ipsius sunt
Quoniam ipsius est mare et ipse fe
cit illud: et siccam manus eius forma
uerunt
Venite adoremus et procidamus et
ploremus ante dominum qui fecit
nos: quia ipse est dominus deus nost.
Et nos populus pascue eius: et oues
manus eius
Hodie si uocem eius audieritis: no
lite obdurare corda uestra
Sicut in irritacione: secundum die

One of the most reliable methods of dating ancient manuscripts is radiocarbon dating (C14 dating). This technique can be used to date materials up to 60,000 years old, but the materials must contain some carbon atoms. Radiocarbon dating is the standard dating technique used to date living organisms, since life is carbon based. The theory behind this technique is that all living organisms breathe in air, which contains both atoms of C12, which is stable, and a very small amount of radioactive C14, which is unstable and slowly decays. Living organisms, plants, and animals constantly take in C12 and C14. C14 is present in much smaller amounts, (that is, millions of times

▲ Here a present day researcher is shown working on a scroll that has been subjected to radiocarbon dating.

smaller), and these levels remain constant in the organism as long as it is alive. When the organism dies, whether plant or animal, it stops taking in or absorbing C12 and C14 and this unstable isotope starts to disintegrate at a constant rate. Its rate of disintegration is indicated by its half-life, which is the time it takes for half of it to break down into other atoms. The half-life of C14 is 5,730 years. Therefore, if an organism had 100 molecules of C14 in its body when it died, in 5,730 years it would have about half of that, which is 50 molecules. Thus, by measuring this ratio in a carbon-based organism, we can extrapolate back and determine when it died and therefore date the material. That is how the Dead Sea Scrolls and other manuscripts were dated. Since they were written on animal skins or papyrus made from plants, the C14 method of dating could be used to discover the approximate date at which the plants were cut down and died. There is a range of error of several hundred years, but radiocarbon is considered to be very reliable for archeological artifacts that are carbon-based. Therefore, we have a very powerful tool for dating ancient artifacts.

When this process was first developed a large portion of any material had to be destroyed in order to carbon date it. No one at that time wanted to destroy a large piece of the scrolls, so in 1952, some of the linen fabric that the scrolls were wrapped in (from Cave 1) was used for carbon dating. The dates arrived at by this method were between 167 B.C.–A.D. 233. By the 1990s, a more efficient technique had been developed, known as the Accelerator Mass Spectrometry (AMS). This new method could carbon date with much less material and with a greater accuracy, that is, a smaller time interval. This time eight scroll fragments were dated and the range was close to the dates expected (200 B.C.–A.D. 100).

▼ Scholars were able to use a blank, albeit rare, piece of papyrus found amongst the scrolls for carbon dating.

◀ The latest equipment for researching the scroll texts us advanced x-ray fluorescence analysis.

5 Samples of Scroll Texts

KEY DOCUMENTS HAVE GIVEN NEW INSIGHTS INTO THE RELIGIOUS COMMUNITY IN QUMRAN, AND HAVE AT THE SAME TIME RAISED INTRIGUING QUESTIONS ABOUT KEY TEACHINGS OF THE JEWISH AND CHRISTIAN FAITHS.

Introduction

Modern Bibles contain 150 Psalms that are attributed to King David. It is fascinating that there are Psalms in the Dead Sea Scrolls that are not present in the Bibles. Some of these Psalms are also attributed to King David, but we were not aware of them until the discovery of the scrolls. All of the known Psalms were also found in the scrolls, but in some sections they occur in a different order (Psalms 107–150). It is very exciting to have discovered previously unknown Psalms in the Dead Sea Scrolls that did not make it into our current Bibles and would otherwise have been lost. Now, because of the discovery of the Dead Sea Scrolls, we have the opportunity to read them.

Psalm seeking forgiveness and deliverance (from Cave 11)

Indeed, no worm gives You thanks, nor any weevil recounts Your loving-kindness.

► An example of one of the Psalm scrolls, found in Cave 11, which was found to contain a number of both canonical and apocryphal psalms.

◄ A 14th century Psalter, which depicts King David playing a harp and composing psalms.

"The living, the living, they thank You," they of uncertain step give You praise when You make them know Your mercy, when You teach them Your righteousness. For the soul of all the living is in Your hand, You alone breathe life into flesh. Render to us, O LORD, by Your goodness; according to Your boundless compassion, Your myriad righteous acts. The LORD hears the voice of those who love His name, of His loving-kindness he deprives them not. Blessed be the LORD, worker of righteousness, who crowns the pious with mercy and compassion. My soul clamors to praise Your name, to praise Your loving-kindness with a joyous cry – to tell of Your faithfulness; of praise due to You there is no measure. I was in death's thrall through my sins; my iniquities had sold me to Sheol – but You saved me, O LORD, according to Your boundless compassion, Your myriad righteous acts. I, too, have loved Your name and throw myself on Your mercy. Forgive, O LORD, my sins, cleanse me from my iniquities! Favor me with a constant and knowing spirit and let me not be shamed by ruin. Let Satan have no dominion over me, nor an unclean spirit; let neither pain nor the will of evil rule in me. Surely You, O LORD, are my praise; in You I place my hope all the day. My brothers rejoice with me, and my father's house, amazed at Your favor! […] I shall be glad in You forever.

(*THE DEAD SEA SCROLLS, A NEW TRANSLATION*, WISE, ABEGG, AND COOK)

The Damascus Document

One of the more interesting texts is called the "Damascus Document." It is a collection of the practices, rules, and regulations of the community. This is a document that was not previously known and which sheds much light on the sectarian community. It includes encouragement to be faithful to the faith and community, as well as purification rites, vows, rules for the Sabbath, and other related religious themes. A later examination will look in more detail at the beliefs and practices of the community who wrote the scrolls. The following is a small part of this document.

... with money ... [his means did not] suffice to [return it to him] and the year [for redemption approaches?] ... and may God release him? from his sins. Let not [ ] in one, for it is an abomination.... And concerning what he said, ["When you sell anything to or buy anything from] your neighbor, you shall not defraud one another," this is the expli[cation ...] everything that he knows that is found ... and he knows that he is wronging him, whether it concerns man or beast.

▼ A section of the Damascus Scroll, which sheds much light on the activities of the sectarian community in Qumran.

▲ Only a small part of the War Rule was found in Cave 1, but it is nonetheless fascinating in that it talks of the sons of light and darkness that are active in the world.

The War Rule

Another previously unknown document is the "War Rule." It talks about a Prince of the Congregation who will be killed or pierced. Only six lines of this text have survived.

Isaiah the prophet: [The thickets of the forest] will be cut [down with an axe and Lebanon by a majestic one will f]all. And there shall come forth a shoot from the stump of Jesse [ ] the Branch of David and they will enter into judgment with [ ] and the Prince of the Congregation, the Bran[ch of David] will kill him [by stroke]s and by wounds. And a Priest [of renown (?)] will command [the s]lai[n] of the Kitti[m]

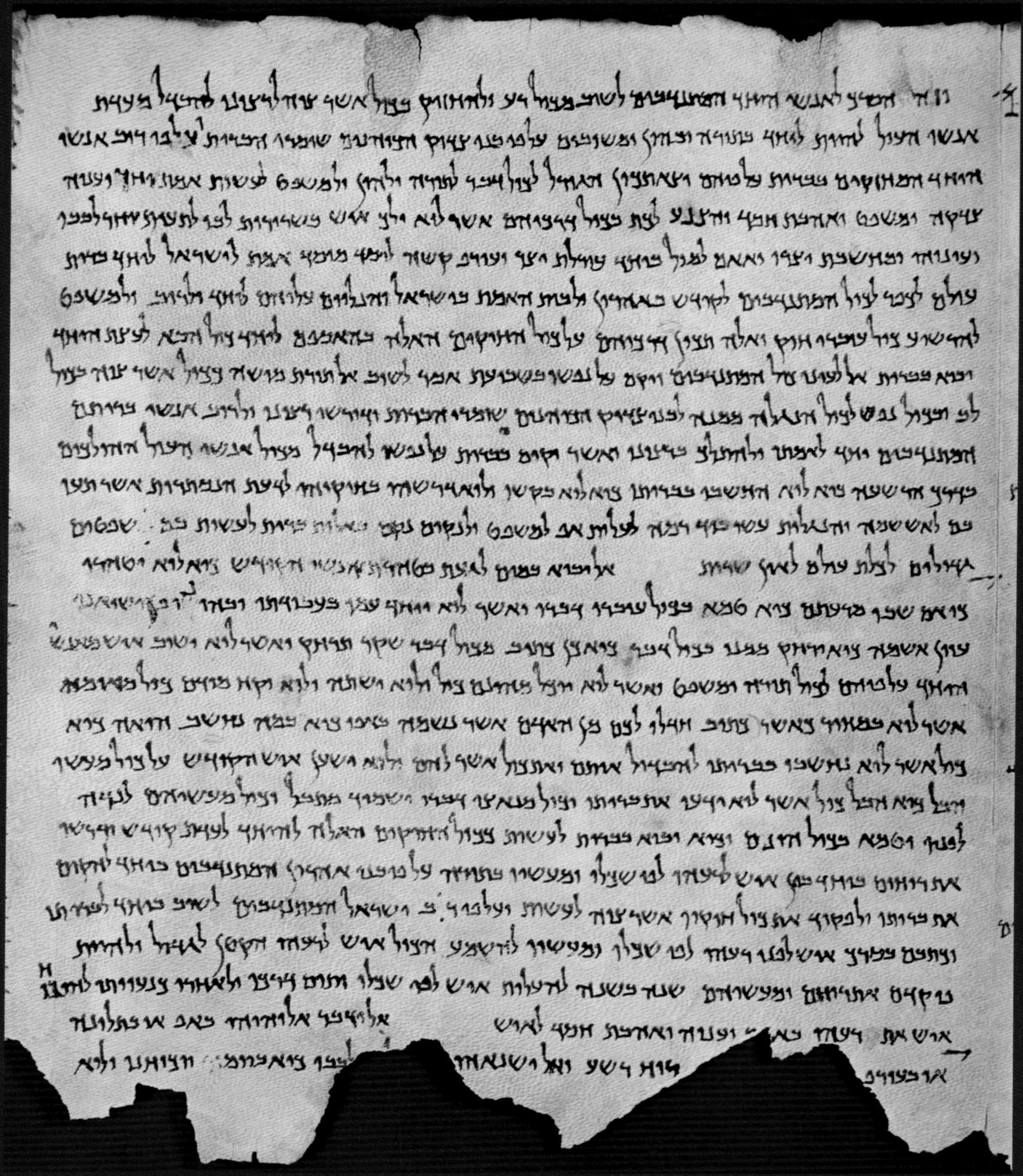

The Community Rule

"The Community Rule," also known as "The Manual of Discipline," is very interesting in that it gives us some insight into the practices of the community. It is basically a set of regulations for those who accept the life of this community to follow. It also gives punishments for those who do not obey the rules.

▼ The importance of reading the Torah is stressed in The Rule of the Community. Here, in a 13th century illustration, King Solomon is seen at study.

And according to his insight he shall admit him. In this way both his love and his hatred. No man shall argue or quarrel with the men of perdition. He shall keep his council in secrecy in the midst of the men of deceit and admonish with knowledge, truth and righteous commandment those of chosen conduct, each according to his spiritual quality and according to the norm of time. He shall guide them with knowledge and instruct them in the mysteries of wonder and truth in the midst of the members of the community, so that they shall behave decently with one another in all that has been revealed to them. That is the time for studying the Torah (lit. clearing the way) in the wilderness. He shall instruct them to do all that is required at that time, and to separate from all those who have not turned aside from all deceit.

◀ Text of The Community Rule, which has given scholars great insight into the workings of the Essene community in Qumran.

▲ An 18th century depiction of Jeroboam worshipping a Gold Calf. The Temple scroll addresses God's covenant with his people to cease their pagan practices.

The Temple Scroll

"The Temple Scroll" is considered by many to be a supplement to the Pentateuch, the first five books of Moses. It is mainly concerned with the temple, its construction and ritual sacrifices. Many are familiar with temple rituals from the book of Leviticus. It is a book that experts believe was not composed by the community associated with the Dead Sea Scrolls, but predates it to about the fifth century B.C. and may have been composed by priests just after the return of the exiles from Babylon.

To summarize, it begins by God addressing the Hebrew nation and making it clear that in his covenant with his people, he expects them to separate themselves from their pagan neighbors. God alone is to be worshipped and not the many gods that their surrounding neighboring countries believe in. This is a conditional covenant and if the Hebrews want to remain free, they will have to follow this rule about only worshipping the one God of Israel. There are also instructions for building the temple, for worship, and how this worship is to be carried out. It appears that this temple will be more magnificent than the one built by Solomon. The text goes into great detail regarding its description and furnishings. It describes three courtyards, not two as in the Bibles. In fact, the third one is so large that it seems unlikely that it was meant to be constructed. Its dimensions would make this courtyard as large as the entire city of Jerusalem. There are laws regarding festivals, sacrifices, purity, and all the rituals the priests would be associated with. This text also states that at the end time God would replace this temple. It would be replaced by one from heaven.

▼ A 19th century engraving depicting Saul responding to the appeals of the people of Gad and Reuben to protect them from the attacks of Nahash.

Previously Unknown Biblical Scrolls

It is always exciting to discover information in the Dead Sea Scrolls that makes some of the Bible stories more understandable. Many Bible stories seem fragmented and incomplete, but certain texts from the Dead Sea Scrolls fill in the gaps and now the stories makes perfect sense.

Two examples in the Bible are the story in I Samuel concerning Nahash, king of the Ammonites, which does not seem to make sense until we read the additional text in the Scrolls explaining Saul's response to an appeal from the people of Gad and Reuben to protect them from the attacks of Nahash. Similarly, in Genesis Chapter 12, there appears to be no explanation of Abraham's decision to travel to Egypt from Canaan until we read in The Dead Sea Scrolls that he had a prophetic dream directing him to do this.

Mystical Dead Sea Scrolls

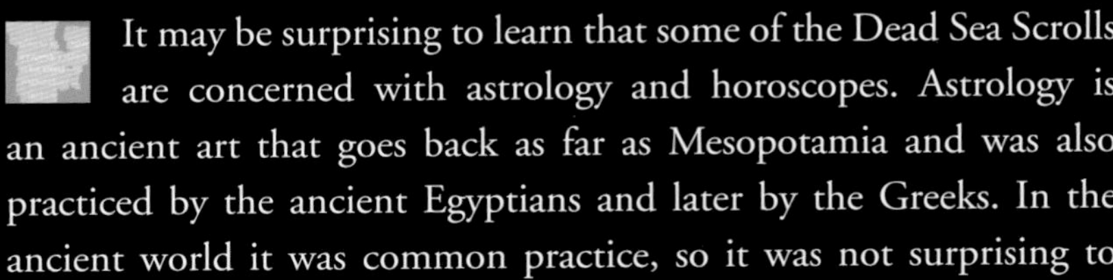

It may be surprising to learn that some of the Dead Sea Scrolls are concerned with astrology and horoscopes. Astrology is an ancient art that goes back as far as Mesopotamia and was also practiced by the ancient Egyptians and later by the Greeks. In the ancient world it was common practice, so it was not surprising to find these texts. Interrelated with astrology is physiognomy, a type of divination which is the art or practice of determining a person's inner character, personality, or traits based on his exterior looks and appearance. Usually it involved observing the physical features of an individual's face and head and correlating these with the person's character traits. These features could include bumps on the head, color of the eyes, hair, and skin, sound of the voice, and the shape of the body. Sometimes it was even used to predict the person's future or destiny. Since, in the ancient world, astrology and physiognomy were not considered pseudoscience, but science itself, you could consider these texts as scientific at the time they were written.

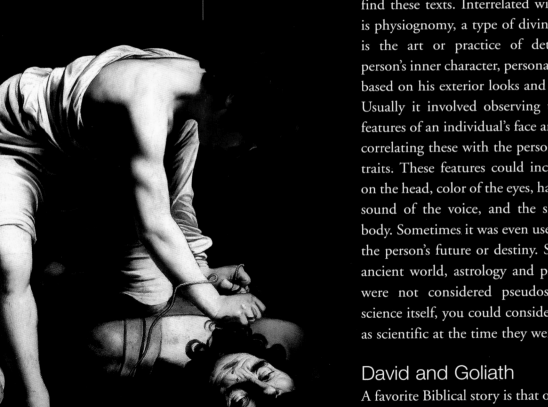

▼ The death of Goliath at the hands of David in the famous painting Caravaggio, in which Goliath is interestingly shown to be a very large man, rather than the giant of legend.

David and Goliath

A favorite Biblical story is that of David and Goliath, which is contained in 1 Samuel 17. David, a mere boy, was going to do battle with the giant Goliath. In verse 4, we can ascertain that Goliath was almost 10 feet tall; according to the *Archeological Study Bible*, 2005, p. 421 the Hebrew term was six cubits and a span which translates to about 3 meters or 9.84 feet. Was this an exaggeration? Let us look to the scrolls for a parallel text. In the Dead Sea Scrolls version of Samuel, 4QSam, the height of Goliath is about four cubits and a span (not six) which is about 2 meters or 6 ½ feet. This would be within the normal range of height for a healthy man in our contemporary society.

Angelic Worship

Angelic worship texts are also found in the Dead Sea Scrolls. This theme was prominent in Jewish mysticism, especially during the Middle Ages when there was a renewed interest in the Divine Throne visions. These types of vision or revelation were known as Merkabah, which translates into Divine Throne, and had to do with the vision of seeing God. Ancient Hebrew tradition stated that everyone, provided that they were at least 30 years old, should read these texts, because just by reading them an individual could experience spontaneous visions and mystical experiences.

▲ Ezekiel's mystical vision, of what the earth would be like if God's laws were disregarded, is depicted here in an early engraving.

The book of Ezekiel has a good example of Merkabah. While Ezekiel was in exile in Babylon with other captives, he was transported to heaven and beheld the Divine Throne in a vision. It is described in the first chapter of Ezekiel.

This is interesting because mysticism is a very personal spiritual experience and not a group or community event. Judaism at that time was practiced in a manner which was very much external and usually by public worship in the temple. This may be one of the first indications of mysticism playing an important role in Judaism, thus opening it up to individual mystical practices. This is an idea that most scholars have not recognized or have chosen to ignore. Today many people pursue this type of individual spiritualism.

6 Khirbet Qumran and the Essenes

THE ESSENE SECT DISAPPEARED AFTER THE DESTRUCTION OF THE TEMPLE IN JERUSALEM BY THE ROMANS IN A.D. 70, AND ARCHEOLOGISTS HAVE NOW UNEARTHED A VAST COMPLEX AT THE SITE IN QUMRAN WHERE THE SCROLLS WERE CREATED OVER MANY YEARS.

Introduction

There are certain historical events that should be acknowledged in order to understand the historical context of the Dead Sea Scrolls and who may have been responsible for either writing and/or hiding them.

Historians refer to certain intervals of time in the history of the Jews as the First and Second Temple periods. There were two temples built in Jerusalem during the history of the Jews. King Solomon built the first one in the 10th century B.C. It lasted over 350 years and was destroyed by Nebuchadnezzar in 586 B.C., when he invaded that area and deported most of the inhabitants. Historians refer to this historical period as the First Temple period. The next period began when the Jews returned from exile. King Cyrus allowed them to return to their land from Babylon where they had been held captive for almost 50 years. This return took

▶ The remains of the Jewish stronghold at Masada, which was laid siege to by a Roman army, and which is a place of great symbolism for all Jewish people.

◀ A medieval depiction of the building of the Temple of Solomon, which was destroyed in 586 B.C.

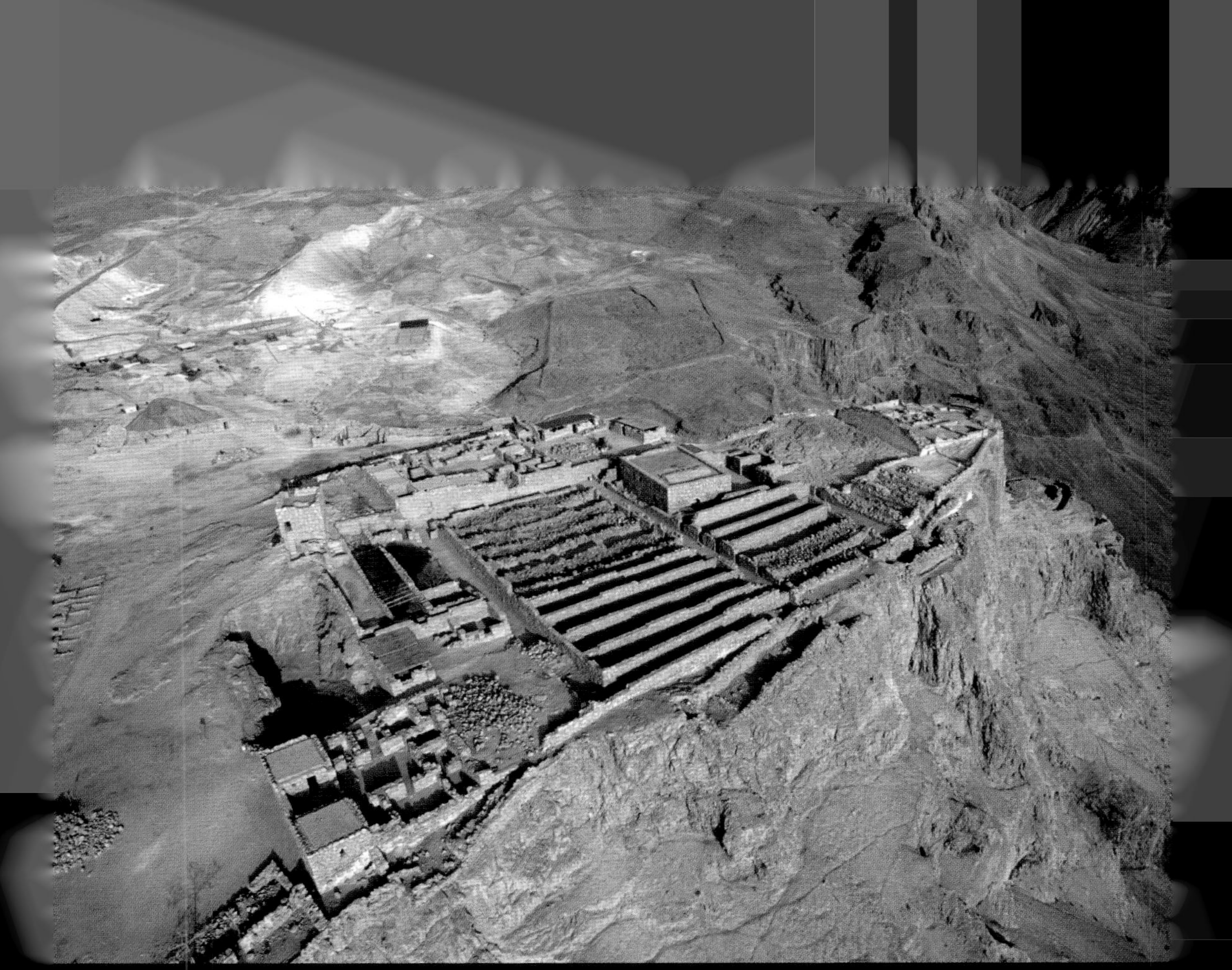

place around 540 B.C. and the temple was rebuilt and restored by the Jews in 515 B.C. The period beginning 515 B.C. was the Second Temple period, which ended with the destruction of Jerusalem by the Romans in A.D. 68. There were several revolts during this period. One was a revolt led by the Maccabeans, around 165 B.C., against the Seleucid Empire. Later, in around A.D. 66, the Judeans revolted against the Romans, and it was not until A.D. 70 that the Temple in Jerusalem was finally totally destroyed. The lingering stronghold of Masada was overrun by the Romans in A.D. 74, thus ending the rebellion. The Jews have always wanted to build a third temple in the same location as the first two, but this has never happened because the place where many believe the first two temples were built is in Arab territory. Many Jews pray for the day when it will be possible to build the temple for the third time.

Discovering the authors

It appears that after the Romans destroyed the Second Temple and the remaining strongholds of the Jewish Rebellion in 70 A.D., the Sadducees and the Essenes disappeared and the only Jewish sect to survive was the Pharisees. This type of Judaism has survived until the present day and is known as Rabbinic Judaism. The other form of religion, that also survived, was Christianity.

To determine who the actual writers of the scrolls were and where they lived, we need to know when they flourished and whether this date is consistent with the dating of the scrolls. Several methods have been used in determining the dates of the scrolls, including paleographic (handwriting analysis), the dating of archeological artifacts found in the caves and at Qumran, and most sophisticated of all, radiocarbon, or C14, dating. All of these methods concur that the scrolls were written sometime between 200 B.C. and A.D. 100. It should be mentioned that the first C14 dating was done in 1950,

▼ Israeli soldiers of the Ultra Orthodox battalion pray at the hilltop fortress of Masada in a ceremony forming part of their graduation.

◄ A medieval illustration from the History of Antiquities, written by Flavius Josephus in the first century A.D., depicting the surrender of the Jewish people to the Roman Emperor Titus in 66 A.D.

but we have now much better and more accurate C14 testing and this also confirms those same dates. The new technique, called AMS (Accelerator Mass Spectrometry), was used in 1990. Historically, we need to see which groups lived in that region during this period. We know the major Jewish sects that existed during that time period, since they were written about by Josephus (A.D. 37–c.100), Philo (20 B.C.–A.D. 50), and Pliny the Elder (A.D. 23–79). These sects were the Pharisees, Sadducees, and the Essenes. Also, from their descriptions by these writers, we can most likely eliminate the first two from responsibility for the scrolls, so that leaves the Essenes as a possibility. Let us look at the actual historical description of the Essenes by these ancient writers and compare that to what the scrolls tell us of their community.

▼ Pliny the Elder's Natural History, written the first century A.D., makes mention of the Essene community in Palestine.

C. PLINII
SECVNDI NATVRALIS
HISTORIAE LIBER
SECVNDVS.

The history of the Essenes

Before the discovery of the Dead Sea Scrolls, we had some description of the Essenes through the writings of two first-century Jewish historians, Josephus and Pliny.

The first, Josephus, is mainly known for his *History of Antiquities* and *History of the Jews*. He says this about the Essenes in his *History of Antiquities*:

"As for the Pharisees, they say that certain events are the work of Fate, but not all … The sect of the Essenes, however, declares that Fate is mistress of all things, and that nothing befalls men unless it be in accordance with her decree. But the Sadducees do away with Fate, holding … that all things lie within our own power …"

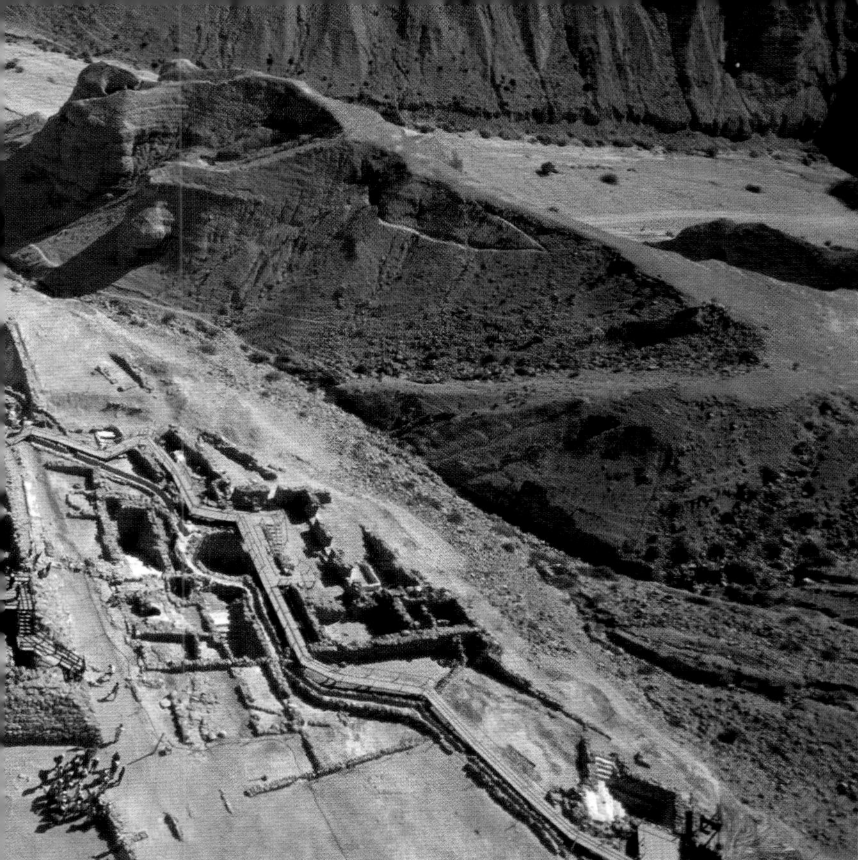

◀ Remains of the extensive settlement at Khirbet Qumran close to the Dead Sea, which was active from 130 B.C.

It says that the Essenes adhered to the principle that everything in this world was ordained by fate. The Sadducees, on the other hand, did not believe in this extreme doctrine of fate but more in free will, and the Pharisees were somewhere in between the belief of the Sadducees and the Essenes. They believed that some things were determined by fate, and others were not.

The Roman geographer, Pliny the Elder also wrote about this community and mentioned the Essenes in his *Natural History*.

On the west side of the Dead Sea ... is the solitary tribe of the Essenes, which is remarkable beyond all the other tribes in the whole world, as it has no women and has renounced all sexual desire, has no money, and has only palm trees for company. Day by day the throng of refugees is recruited to an equal

number by numerous accessions of persons tired of life and driven thither by the waves of fortune to adopt their manners. Thus through thousands of ages … an age in which no one who is born lives on forever: so prolific for their advantage is other men's weariness of life! Lying below the Essenes was formerly the town of Engedi, second only to Jerusalem in the fertility of its land and in its groves of palm trees, but now like Jerusalem a heap of ashes.

▼ Steps leading down to the water supply at Qumran. Archeologists are unsure whether this was for the supply of domestic water only, or for bathing and baptism.

At first glance, it does appear that the scrolls describe their community in very similar terms to the description of the Essenes by these first century historians. There is much consistency as regards their location, the west side of the Dead Sea, and their beliefs and practices. With this information from the ancient historians and

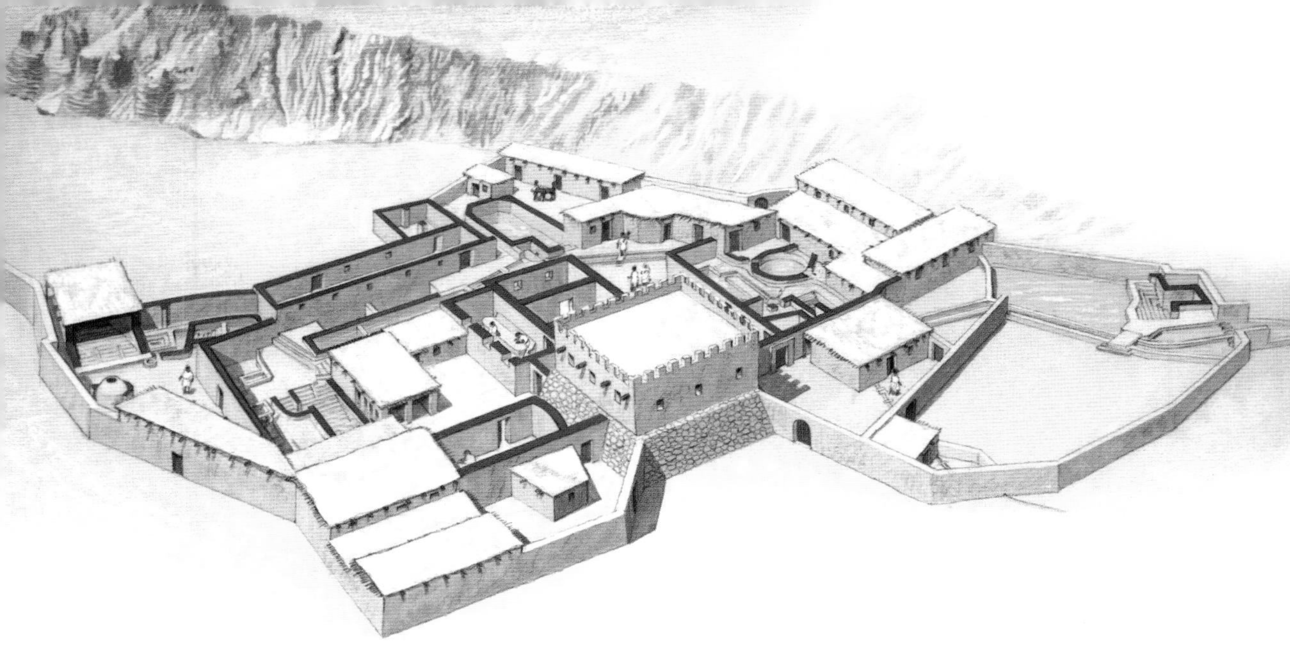

▲ An artist's impression of the site at Khirbet Qumran showing its extensive buildings, which were eventually destroyed by the Roman army.

the results of the C14 dating, most Dead Sea Scroll scholars believe that the community or sect that lived in this area of the Dead Sea at Khirbet Qumran were the Essenes, and they were the ones who wrote the scrolls and hid them in the caves. Also, archeological artifacts seem to substantiate these claims. However, not everyone accepts this hypothesis, as there are inconsistencies that put it into question and there have been several experts who disagree with the traditional view that the Dead Sea Scrolls were written, and hidden in the caves, by the Essene community that lived at Qumran. We will be looking at some of the theories that purport that the Essenes had nothing to do with the Dead Sea Scrolls.

What do we know about this group known as the Essenes? The beginnings of an answer can be found by considering the archeological site. To begin with, the complete name of this particular archeological site is Khirbet Qumran. The term Khirbet is Arabic for "ruin" so Khirbet Qumran means "the ruin of Qumran." For brevity, scholars usually just use the term "Qumran" to refer to this site.

▲ An artist's impression of a scribe at work in the scriptorium at Qumran. It is evident from the differing writing that a large number of scribes were employed at one time or another.

This archeological site, or ruin, is located on the northwest shore of the Dead Sea. It was probably built between 130 B.C. and 100 B.C. An earthquake that occurred around 31 B.C. destroyed much of this site. It was rebuilt by 4 B.C. and eventually destroyed by the Romans in A.D. 68.

From excavations in this area, many believe that there was a central location in which about 200 members of this sect lived. Other members may have inhabited the surrounding caves and areas. It is believed that the members of this community ate common meals at the central location. This would also have been the gathering points for rituals, meetings, and community events. One of the most important and interesting archeological finds in the Qumran ruins are tables that could actually have been used to write many of the scrolls. Also discovered were underground water systems, which may have been used for drinking purposes and possibly baptizing rituals.

One of the most puzzling finds is that, if this community had written most of the scrolls, you would expect most to be written in the same, or a few, hands, as it is likely that only the scribes would write or copy them. Not everyone was a scribe and there were limited numbers of them; each scribe would probably have copied many books. However, for some reason, a few books were copied by the same hand or scribe and about a dozen books that were copied were found to have been written by the same hand. All of the rest were in different hands. This is puzzling, but one possible explanation might be that many of the books came from other sources and were added to the library of books that they had copied and composed themselves.

Making the Qumran Connection

The first realization that the scrolls from the caves, and the ruins of Qumran, were related came as early as the 1950s. This theory was first proposed by the Catholic priest, Roland de Vaux, who was one of the first to excavate and explore Qumran, from 1953–1956. The view has been challenged, but most scholars believe the overwhelming evidence that this site of Khirbet Qumran was occupied by the Essenes during that time (200 B.C. to A.D. 68), and that they were responsible for writing some of the Dead Sea Scrolls and for hiding them. In fact, Cave 4 is extremely close to Qumran and many of the others are not far away, thus increasing the evidence for the relationship.

◄ Father Roland Vaux, the Catholic priest who was one of the first people to excavate the site at Khirbet Qumran in the early 1950s and to suggest that it was there that the scrolls were written.

It has been ascertained from the sectarian scroll texts that the description of the Essenes community by several first century historians, including Josephus, Philo, and Pliny the Elder, is fairly consistent with the location and beliefs of the Qumran community. Pliny the Elder's brief description of the location is very similar to the location in which the ruins of Qumran are found. Also, the pottery unearthed at Qumran has been dated to the same time as the scrolls. In fact, some of the potsherds that have been found at Qumran and which have writing on them appear to match the style of the writing on some of the scrolls.

The Qumran Site

It appears that not all of the members of this sect lived on the Qumran ruins site. Some have estimated the number in this community and it is clear that the site would not have been large enough to house them all. It is believed that many people of this community lived in caves and tents surrounding the Qumran site. The Qumran center would have acted as a central place for rituals, meetings, meals, ritual baths, and festivals. At first, many scholars believed that all the members of the Essenes were celibate males, but many now believe that there were also married members, who probably lived in nearby towns and not at the site or surrounding it. Thus, there may have been two groups of Essenes, one celibate and the other married.

▼ Examples of domestic pottery found at the site in Qumran and dated in the first century A.D. by archeologists.

In the ruins, several separate areas have been identified. One is a large area called the refectory, which may have served as a dining room and probably included several rows of tables. In a nearby room, over a thousand utensils were uncovered which included cups, bowls, and plates. Another and more interesting room was found lined with benches and inkwells. This may have served as an area for writing, possibly for writing some of the Dead Sea Scrolls, and was called the scriptorium. Many believe it was located on the second floor of this building built by the Essenes. It must be clarified that no scrolls were ever found in the ruins of Qumran, so the link is mainly from the archeological artifacts found and historical records. Also, consistent with this theory, archeologists believe that they have found the ritual baths that the Essenes used and evidence of how they channeled water to this location using aqueducts. These baths were in the shape of large stepped cisterns. Some experts challenge the ritual bath theory and think they were just storage areas for water. Thousands of tombs have also been found in several cemeteries at Qumran but only some have been excavated. In addition, a potter's workshop, a flour mill, and other areas have been identified.

Since coins, pottery, glass, and other items were found at Qumran, many feel the community did not live in complete isolation but at least traded with others.

▼ The outer walls of the scriptorium at Qumran, in which the remains of benches, on which scribes would have been seated whilst writing the scrolls, have been discovered.

The Qumran Community

Before the Qumran site was destroyed by the Romans in A.D. 68, it was a peaceful settlement. It appears that this group first moved to this site from Jerusalem to establish their community. They must have chosen this area because it was a solitary place that would give them privacy and separate them from the outside world. They could practice their community's way of life without interference from others. At that time, many individuals, groups, and sects sought the desert and wilderness to lead a solitary religious life, since they believed it was a perfect place to seek God, pray, and meditate.

▼ Scholars can still only speculate about the exact character of the people who inhabited Khirbet Qumran. But it is certain that, like the hermits of the Middle Ages, many chose to set themselves apart from the main community.

There was a hierarchical structure, as indicated by the seating arrangements in the assemblies mentioned in the scrolls. At the head of this structure was the master, then the priests, elders, and the rest of the congregation. There was a chief financial officer called the mebaqqer who managed the money and property of the congregation. Any earnings of the novices were given to the mebaqqer.

There was also a council, made up of 12 members and three priests. It is not known for sure what they were in charge of, but it has been suggested that they decided the legal matters of the congregation, so maybe this was their version of our courts and legal system. Since they had many religious and secular rules, it is possible that this court heard violations and gave out punishments.

If someone wanted to become a member of this community, he had to have a two- to three-year initiation period. Scholars differ on whether it was two or three years but, in either case, this was a probationary time during which a prospective member could leave before he made any formal commitments. He would be taught the rules of the community, trained, and educated during this period, and would gradually be integrated into the community. It was during his second year that the candidate would turn over all his possessions and money to the community.

▲ Throughout history there have been examples of religious groups who have cut themselves off from society, such as the group of 19th century nuns shown here.

Experts disagree, but it does appear that the main community at the site was composed mainly, if not exclusively, of men, who were probably celibate. There is some evidence, however, that some women, and even children, may have been part of, or at least interacted with, the community. Remains of some women and children have been found in the Qumran burial sites, but this could also be explained in other ways.

Most experts now believe that the married members did not live at Qumran main site but lived in camps or towns throughout the area. These members had children and were probably employed in various occupations in the town or village in which they lived. They were required to follow many of the rules of the community but had some flexibility in this matter. They were instructed by priests from the community. Even though they lived separately, there were considered part of the community. Therefore, based on the descriptions by ancient writers and the Dead Sea Scrolls, it appears that the main characteristics and beliefs of this community were as follows:

First, they were separatists. They obviously decided to remove themselves from society and live in a remote and secluded site. That did not mean they wanted to eliminate all contact with the outside world, since it appears from the artifacts recovered that they did engage in trade. Similarly, today, there are groups that choose to accept this way of life, such as cloistered nuns, who try to remain secluded from society.

Another main characteristic is that they shared everything; that is, had everything in common. Besides sharing their possessions, as they believed they did not own anything personally but that the community owned it, they shared their meals, work, and just about everything else. Their lives were lived in simplicity. They ate simple foods and wore simple or plain clothes. Regarding their prayer life, it appears that they prayed together as a community at least twice a day. They did not own slaves or believe in slavery.

In terms of their religious beliefs they held some similar beliefs to the Pharisees of their time but there were also differences. They believed in one God, in angels, in the Torah and in many ideas taken directly from the Bible, and in a life of purity. They also believed in good and evil, as they considered themselves the Sons of Light and would oppose the Sons of Darkness. They also believed in a messiah. Actually, they believed in the coming of two messiahs, one who would be political and one who would be their priest messiah. They also practiced some forms of astrology. The degree to which they believed in this or practiced it is unknown, but at that time it would not have been uncommon. They did not follow or observe the practices of the Temple in Jerusalem as they felt these were distorted and corrupt.

It must be pointed out that on reading the scrolls, it is apparent that they believed in a Divine plan and that God was in control of everything. Even evil was under the control and plan of God and in the end, God would intervene and they would become victorious. This is similar to the theme of the Christian book of Revelation. Thus, in a sense, they were determinists. They also believed the battle between Good and Evil spirits occurred not only on the earth but in the spirit or angelic realm. This has many similarities to New Testament thoughts on the battle between good and evil and the end times. Because of their deterministic views, they also believed more

▶ The community at Qumran shared many beliefs with their contemporaries, such as the Pharisees, and although the scrolls that archeologists have retrieved are not as exotic as the Torah illustrated here, they would nevertheless have been highly valued.

אנכי ה
לא יהיה
לא תשא
זכור את
כבד את
לא תרצח
לא תנאף
לא תגנב
לא תענה
לא תחמד

▲ It is clear that the authors of the scrolls believed in a Divine plan where God is in direct contact with the Earth, as in the New Testament Book of Revelation, from which this illustration is taken.

strongly than the other Jewish sects that God would intervene in world affairs. They believed their community had a major role to play in this conflict and I guess they considered themselves special or chosen to carry out this task.

The community had leaders. There was a master, a council, and an entire community. New members were accepted once a year and on a specific day. Also at this time, old members renewed their pledges. Their calendar differed from the Jewish religious calendar, which was lunar and based only on the moon, whereas their calendar was also based on the sun.

Interesting rules that we read about from the Dead Sea Scrolls include spitting. They were not supposed to spit to the right or the middle of people.

Esoteric Connections

There is one thing mentioned in the scrolls which I think scholars have ignored because they are not well versed in this area: I believe that the Essenes practiced a form of angelic invocation. Most scroll scholars point out that they were interested in esoteric teachings and invoked the names of angels. They usually go no further than this. Angelic communication goes back as far as the beginning of man and this one practice may have distinguished them from the Pharisees and scribes of their times. It does seem that one of the reasons they separated themselves from the world was that they believed they would be joined by angels to fight the last apocalyptic battle on earth. These angels or Heavenly Hosts were real to them and they had every expectation of them coming to their aid. In the War Scroll there is mention of the angels joining them in the wilderness.

Other esoteric areas they may have practiced include divination or prophecy, the use of herbs, and a type of spiritualism, as they believed there was an afterlife and that the soul continued to live on.

Even though most scroll scholars believe that the Essenes lived at Qumran and were responsible for the Dead Sea Scrolls, not all agree. There are dissenters who say that there is just too much evidence that does not fit into the "accepted" theory.

◀ As with later Christian communities, heavenly hosts were clearly very real to the people who wrote the scrolls in Qumran.

Military Scrolls

Some of the scrolls are military or warlike in nature and the Essenes, it is thought, were pacifists or at least a peaceful sect. In fact, some experts speculate that the Qumran site was a military fort. This was proposed by scroll scholar Norman Golb. He believes that rebels who fought against the Roman occupation used the Qumran site as a military base in the first century A.D. A different theory was put forth by Belgian archeologists. They believed it was a kind of winter residence for the rich and powerful. They also believed that the scriptorium was actually a dining room and that the tables within, which were covered with thick plaster, were actually used as dining tables and not by scribes to copy scrolls. The water cisterns, too, could have been used for drinking and washing instead of for ritual baptisms.

▼ The shape of the bath at Qumran suggests that would have lent itself to the ritual of baptism.

Other Questions

The burial of women and children in their cemeteries also raise questions as to who they really were. Were they a celibate society and composed mainly of men? Are there references to John the Baptist, James, Paul, and even Jesus in the Dead Sea Scrolls? Was this a Jewish sect that became, or evolved into, an early Christian sect?

So, with more research and the uncovering of more scrolls and artifacts, we may finally find out for sure who lived at Qumran, who wrote the scrolls, and who hid them in the caves.

◀ Scholars continue to debate what actually took place in Qumran, and its connection with the pre-Christian and post-Crucifixion Christian community, particularly figures like John the Baptist, although to date no specific mention has been found.

7 Artifacts, Cemeteries, Graves and Caves

IN ADDITION TO THE WORK ON DECIPHERING THE SCROLLS, RESEARCHERS HAVE BEEN ABLE TO DISCOVER MUCH MORE ABOUT THE COMMUNITY RESPONSIBLE FOR THEIR CREATION AND THE WAY THAT IT FUNCTIONED.

Introduction

One method used to date the Dead Sea Scrolls is to analyze and date the artifacts found in the ruins of Khirbet Qumran. This is, of course, assuming that the Qumran community had something to do with the scrolls found in the caves. Some of the most numerous artifacts found in the caves and at the Qumran site were of pottery, and fragments of pottery. Examples include jars, vases, and dishes that this community presumably used for cooking, drinking, and eating.

Other artifacts, made of wood, have been retrieved and these lend themselves to C14 dating. They include wooden bowls, combs and boxes. Numerous textiles were also found and have been identified as linen; remember that some of the scrolls were found enrobed in linen cloths. Other artifacts include baskets, stone items coins, and phylactery cases, which are small leather boxes containing small scrolls, with verses of scripture, that were worn on the head and arms. The coins have been identified and dated by numismatic experts, and are consistent with the dates at Qumran and the Dead Sea Scrolls. They are thought to have been minted between about 130–125 B.C.

A particularly interesting archeological nd is a writing instrument that was used t Qumran. Amazingly, the only surviving tylus from Qumran still has traces of dried ık on it. This was the writing instrument sed by the scribes. A bronze inkwell that vas found at Qumran also has residue of ink ı it. The ink was found to be composed of ımpblack, a powdery carbon, and gum.

A copper ink pot, dating from the first to third century D. and similar to those that the scribes in Qumran ould have used.

A phylactery case, made of leather, in which small rolls were held, found at Qumran and dating from the st century A.D.

A ceramic cooking pot dating from the first century D. and found in one of the graves in Qumran.

The Archeological Evidence

The most interesting correlations between the Dead Sea Scrolls and the Qumran site concern the pottery. In the 1950s, it was shown that the pottery at the Khirbet Qumran site matched the pottery in Cave 1 of the Dead Sea Scrolls. This discovery led to greater interest in the Qumran site and sparked its excavation. The Khirbet Qumran site had been known for over a hundred years but there had been little interest in it. In the nineteenth century, archeologists first investigated it to see if this location matched any ancient sites mentioned in the Bible. Since it did not appear to do so, few archeologists were interested in this site until pottery was discovered that matched the pottery from the cave.

► Henry Baker Tristram, an early archeologist who considered the site at Qumran of far less importance than those at Sodom and Gomorrah.

One early explorer of the Qumran site was an English clergyman named Henry Baker Tristram, who was born in 1822. He made several visits to Palestine between 1858 and 1872 for the purpose of searching for the ancient biblical city of Sodom and Gomorrah. Tristram did not find any evidence linking these cities with the Qumran site. In 1872 and 1873, Charles Clermont-Ganneau, a French archeologist and discoverer of the Moabite Stele, explored certain sites in the Palestine area. He excavated several tombs around Jerusalem and one at the Qumran site. He did not believe the Qumran ruins were of any importance and, for the next 150 years, there was no interest in this ancient site from any archeologists.

Recent Discoveries

Modern excavation of the Qumran site has led archeologists to believe there were three different occupations of this site. This conclusion is based on the identification of three different strata levels. By identifying specific pottery, coins, and other artifacts, experts can assign relative dates to the different levels unearthed in which they find these artifacts. Modern archeologists believe the first period of occupation was called the Israelite Phase and was from the eighth to the seventh century B.C. This would have been toward the end of the Kingdom of Israel. The second period is known as the Communal Phase and was the time when many believe the Essenes occupied this area. This ended in A.D. 68 when the Romans destroyed it. It also appears that for several years after this time, the Roman army set up an outpost at Qumran, but that probably ended around A.D. 73. The site was unoccupied for almost 60 years. The third and final period is called the Second Revolt Phase and was from about A.D. 132–135. It is believed that some of the Jews took refuge here from the Roman army during the second Jewish revolt. We are mainly concerned with the Second period known as the Communal Phase when, as many scholars believe, it was occupied by the Essenes.

Cemetries and Graves

The identification and excavation of certain graves at the cemeteries at Qumran is very interesting. Initially, three cemeteries were identified in the Qumran area that are believed to have been used by the Essenes. The largest is the main cemetery and is east of the Qumran site. It appears to have as many as 1,200 graves. There are also two additional smaller cemeteries, one on the north side and one on the south side, which may contain only about 50 burials in each one. Between 1949 and 1955, Roland de Vaux exhumed the first skeletal remains from the Qumran cemeteries. This area was also mapped during the summers of 2001 and 2002. It is a mystery that, in the graves that were excavated, no objects or personal belongings

◄ ▲ Aerial and detailed views of the cemetery at Qumran, where the majority of those buried have been found to be men, and where each grave is covered by a bed of rocks.

were found buried with the bodies. Most of the bodies found were men, although a few graves were found to hold the remains of women and children. Forensic evidence indicated that the age of most of the individuals at the time of death was about 40 years. Interestingly, each grave was found to be covered with a bed of rocks. Some believe that the women's and children's remains were from secondary burials; that is, that they were buried in a much later period.

More recent surveys indicate that there are actually six cemeteries and not three. There are north and south sections of the main cemetery, north, middle and south extensions, and also a cemetery on the north hill.

The Eleven Caves

11 caves have been discovered so far that contained scrolls, fragments, and artifacts that are believed to be associated with the Qumran community, but there may still be undiscovered caves with manuscripts waiting to see the light of day.

Cave One

The first cave, or Cave 1, contained seven intact scrolls as well as pottery jars, fragments of pottery, and some scattered manuscript fragments. This was the first cave to be discovered and it appears that this cave was never entered or opened by anyone until the Bedouin cousins discovered it in 1947. It is believed to have been sealed in the A.D. 60s.

▼ Caves 1 and 2 are shown clearly here, making it surprising that Cave 2 was not entered until five years after the first discovery was made.

Fifty jars have been removed from this cave. Also, by studying and trying to reconstruct the fragments, it appears that originally there were at least 80 intact scrolls present. What happened to them remains a mystery. Some believe that the Bedouin cousins who first entered this cave may have taken many of them and burned them for firewood back at the camp or even sold them on the black market. This is a very real possibility since it is believed that they were the first people to enter the cave after it was sealed, so they could have had something to do with these missing manuscripts. It is also possible that nature, through weather, erosion, and insects, played a part in the disintegration of some of these scrolls. Unfortunately, we may never know the truth of what became of them.

Cave Two

Cave 2 was the second cave to be discovered, not by the Bedouins, who by now knew the value of the scrolls and were searching for more caves, but by the archeologists themselves. They, too, decided to search for additional caves after Cave 1 was discovered. This cave, discovered in 1952 five years after Cave 1 was discovered, contained a few smashed pottery jars and fragments from approximately 40 scrolls. Again, even if just a fragment or two is found from an original scroll, this counts as one of the original 40. Most of these scrolls were texts from the Bible and some were texts of apocryphal books.

Cave Three

Cave 3 was also discovered by archeologists in 1952, the same year that Cave 2 was discovered. The most obvious items found were fragments from broken jars and it is believed

▼ Cave 3 was discovered at the same time as Cave 2. However, judging from the number of empty jars, it would appear that many scrolls had already disappeared. It was here that the Copper Scroll was found.

that originally there were over 30 intact jars present. Very few scroll fragments were found in this cave. In fact, the reconstruction process showed there were probably not more than 25 scrolls originally present here.

The most unusual, or we could say phenomenal, discovery, which received international publicity, was made in this cave. Besides broken jars and scattered scroll fragments, a very unusual copper scroll was discovered. This was the only copper scroll found in any of the caves, and what it contained was very exciting. It was basically a treasure map of 64 locations in the Palestine area in which huge amounts of gold and silver were hidden or buried. The copper scroll was found broken into two pieces. It was very brittle and impossible to open without breaking it.

▼ The unique Copper scroll which has been the subject of so much speculation, referring, as it does, to 64 locations where treasure can be found.

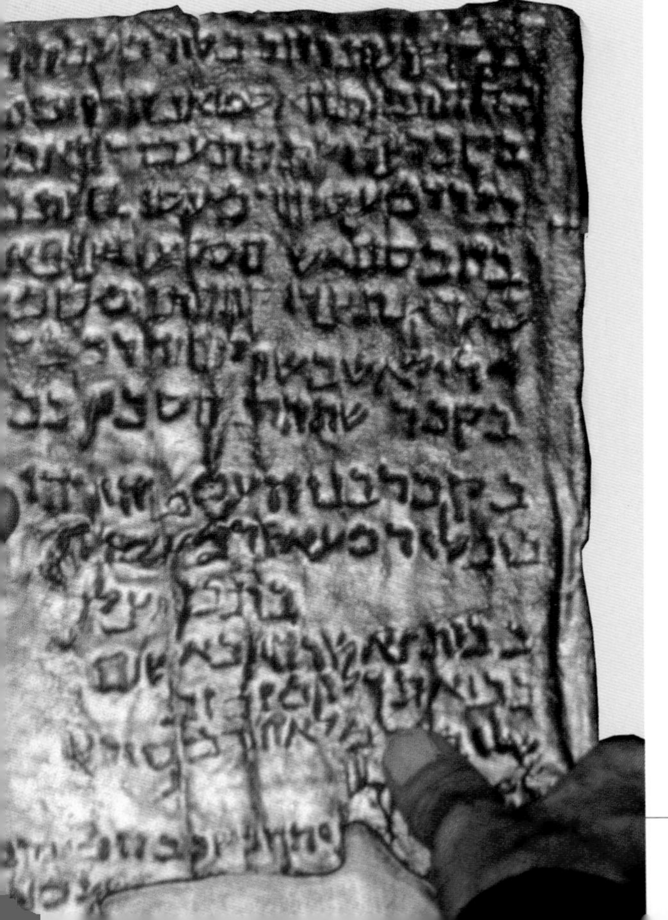

Cave Four

Cave 4, discovered in 1954, was the most significant find in terms of the number of scroll fragments found. This cave was discovered, not by the archeologists, but by a group of Bedouins. They tried to smuggle out the fragments to sell on the black market but were eventually caught and stopped. We do not know how many they managed to sell. The fragments in this cave represented over 560 original scrolls. It took archeologists over six years to remove all the fragments from Cave 4.

Cave Five

Cave 5 was also discovered in 1952, by archeologists. The scroll fragments found here were in very poor condition and fragments representing 30 original scrolls were found.

▲ Cave 4, where it appears that many scrolls were removed by the Bedouin before archeologists were informed of its existence.

Caves 6–10

The Bedouins discovered Cave 6 and few fragments were found here. The number of original scrolls represented was about 35. Few fragments were found in the remaining Caves 7–10.

Cave Eleven

In Cave 11, the longest scroll was found. This was the Temple Scroll. The Bethlehem cobbler and antique dealer, mentioned previously, was found to be hiding a scroll in a shoebox hidden under the floor in his store. It turned out to be the Temple Scroll and this very significant scroll was recovered from him by the Israel Authorities in 1967.

It is not known how many, if any, additional caves may still contain scrolls that are waiting to be discovered. Also, it is unclear just how many were recovered by the Bedouins and whether others may have been sold on the black market.

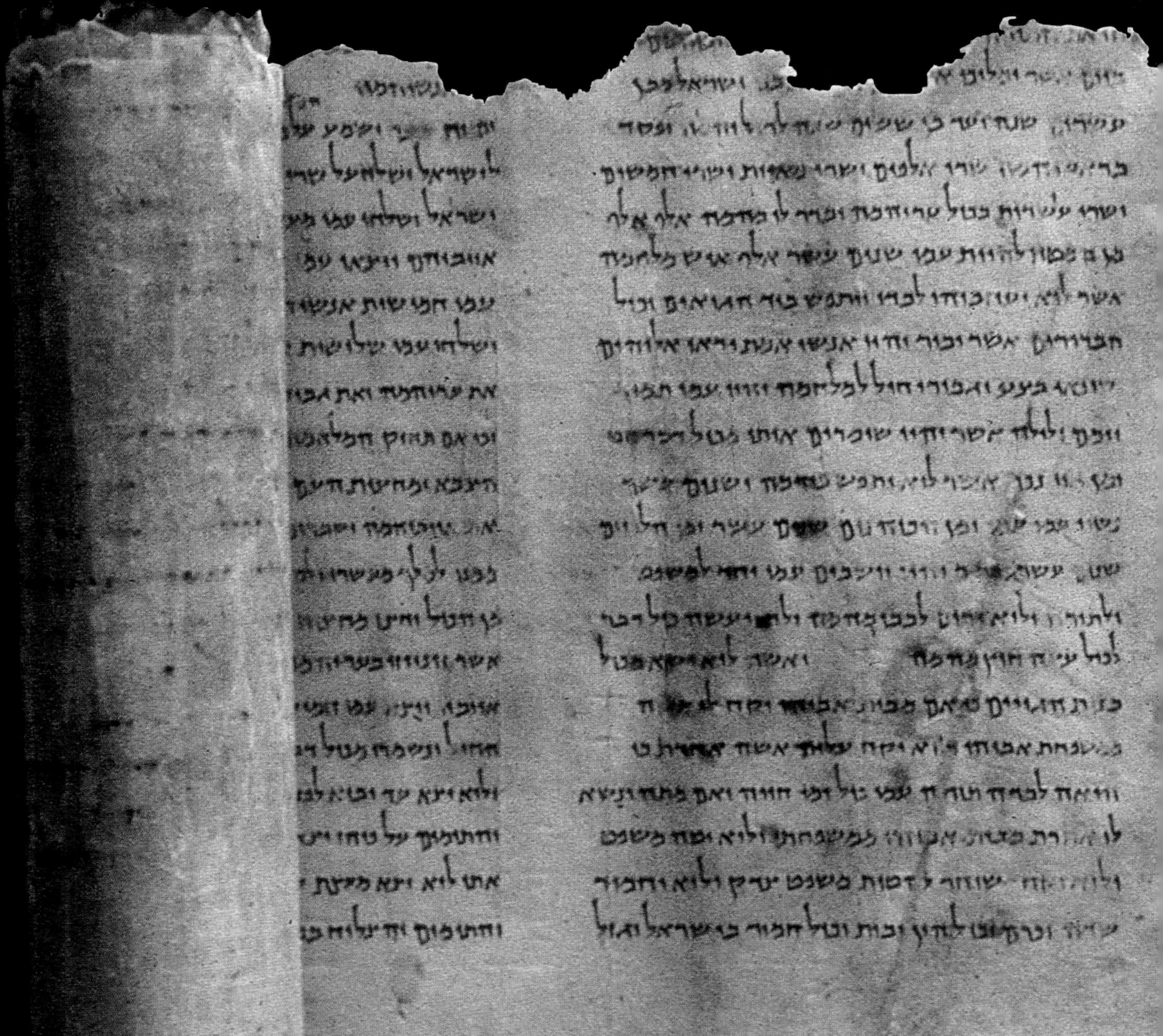

▲ The Temple Scroll, which is the longest single fragment, measuring over 28 feet in length.

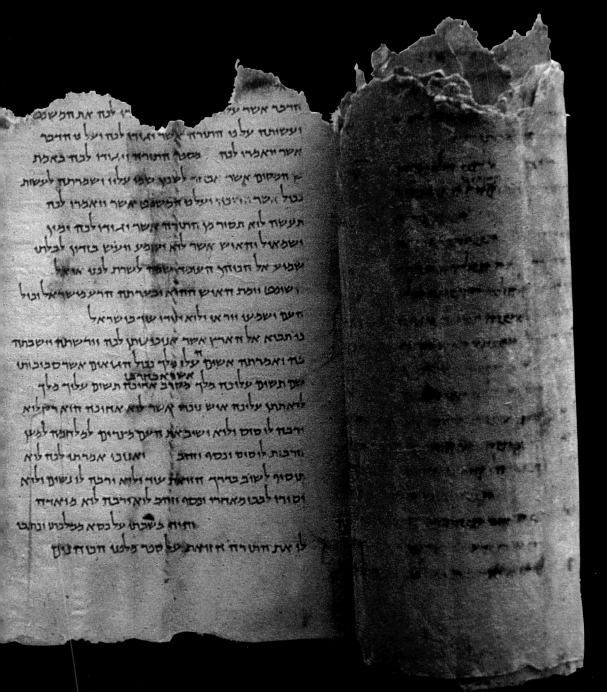

8 The Copper Scroll and the Search for Buried Treasure

PERHAPS THE MOST UNIQUE AND INTRIGUING DISCOVERY WAS A SCROLL CONSTRUCTED, NOT OF PARCHMENT, BUT OF METAL, WHICH ALLUDES TO A TREASURE FAR MORE TANGIBLE THAN SPIRITUAL, AND WHICH CONTINUES TO INTRIGUE SCHOLARS AND WRITERS THE WORLD OVER.

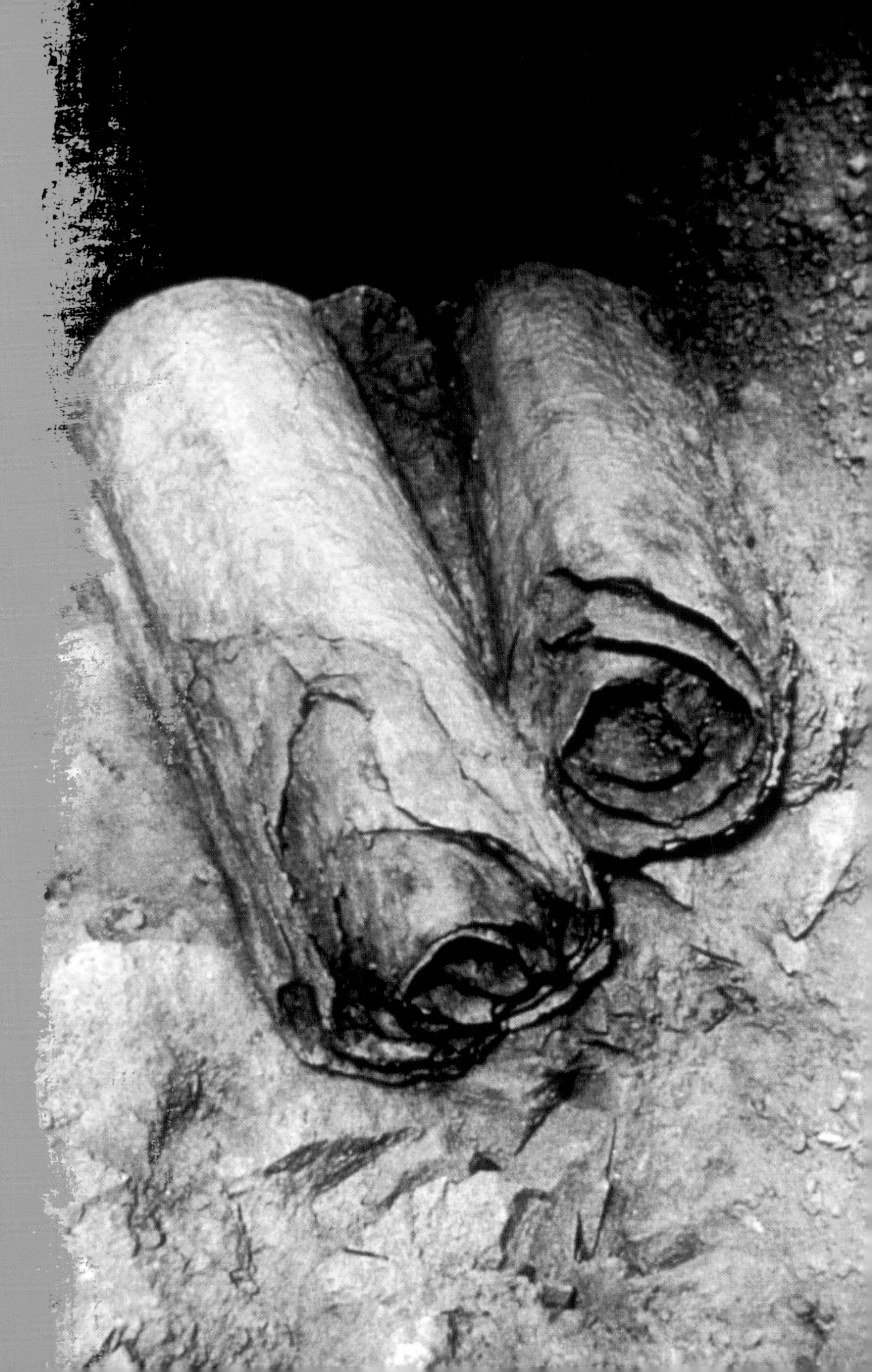

Introduction

There have been many stories and legends regarding the lost treasure of the Knights Templar. This order of Knights existed during the Middle Ages and was considered the military arm of the Roman Catholic Church, and also protected pilgrims during the Crusades. It is speculated that they amassed a vast fortune of treasure. In the fourteenth century, because of jealousy and fear of their growing power, Pope Clement ordered the arrest, torture, and burning at the stake of the members of this order. It is believed that they hid their immense treasure before they were all either killed or dispersed; and to this day it has not been recovered.

In recent years, there has been increasing speculation that the Knights Templar may have discovered a vast treasure beneath their quarters in Jerusalem, which were located within the al-Aqsa mosque above the Old Temple Mount. There has been further speculation that possible reference to this treasure is made in a most unusual scroll found in Cave 3 in Qumran, though so far it seems that this scroll raises more questions than answers.

▶ The last Grand Master of the Templars, Jacques de Molay, and Geoffroi de Charnay are burnt at the stake in 1414 AD.

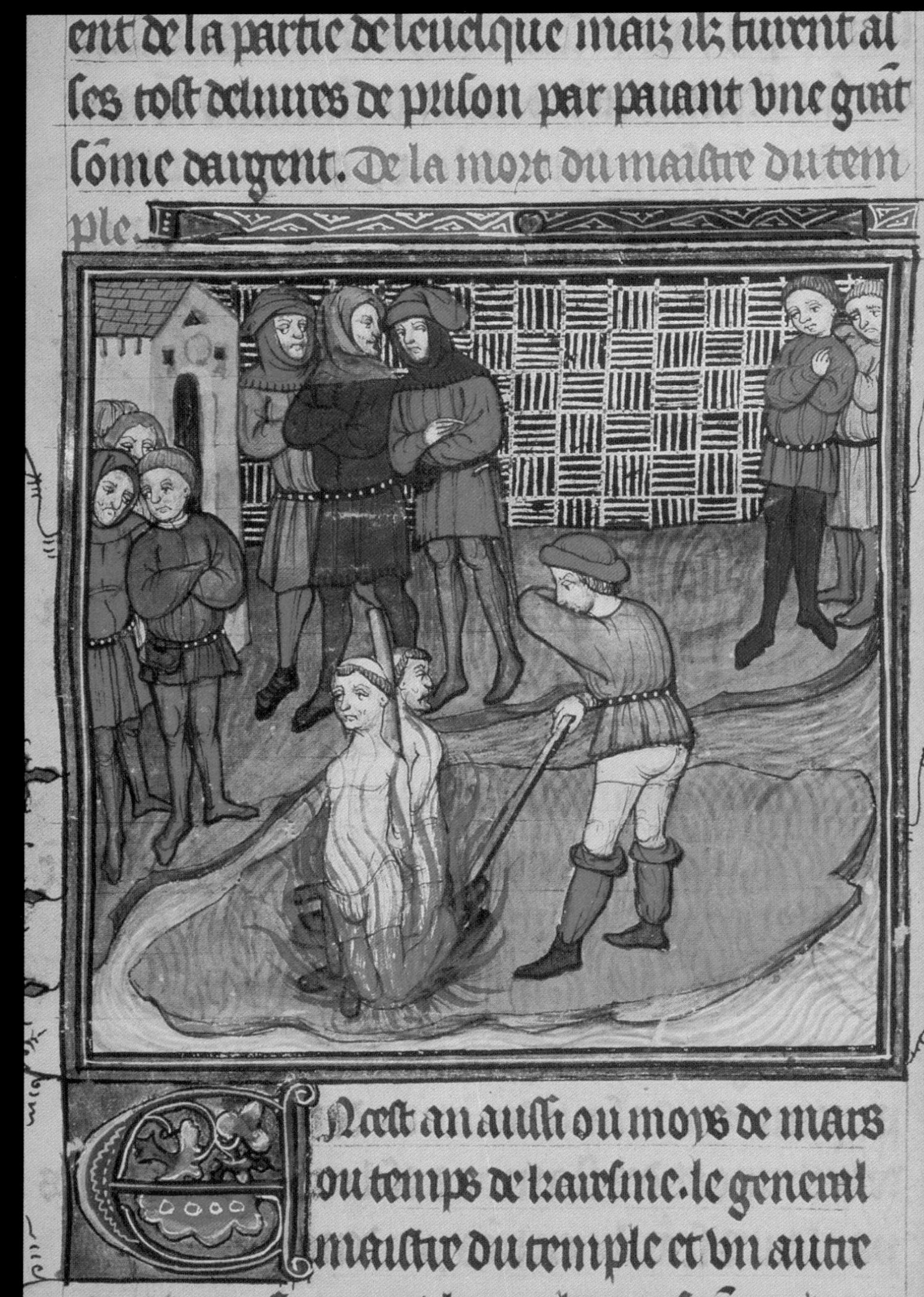

ent de la partie de leuesque maiz ilz furent al
ses tost deliurez de prison par paiant une grant
somme dargent. De la mort du maistre du tem
ple.

En cest an aussi ou moys de mars
ou temps de karesme. le general
maistre du temple et un autre

◀ The Al-Aqsa mosque, which is built on the site of the Temple of Solomon and in the stables of which the original Knights Templar were quartered.

A Unique Discovery

In the spring of 1952, while searching the back of Cave 3, an archeological team discovered two rolled pieces of copper all by themselves. In fact, it was found in the back separate from the other scrolls, pottery, and fragments in that cave. Originally, it was just one copper scroll, but the scroll over time had been broken into two pieces. The scroll was badly oxidized and very brittle, but it had survived this long because the copper content of the metal was extremely high. Pure copper does not oxidize as easily as copper with more alloys or impurities. This was the only copper scroll found in any of the caves and its text revealed something extraordinary. It was written in Hebrew and the letters were probably punched out using a hammer and chisel. There were over 3,000 Hebrew characters making up the scroll. It could not be unrolled easily without it breaking or crumbling so it took a number of years to open it out.

▶ One of twenty-three pieces of the Copper Scroll.

▼ In order that scholars could work on the copper scroll, it was necessary to cut it into 23 narrow strips so that the whole of the text could be revealed.

It had to be cut into strips to get it open so that the text could be read. This was eventually done in 1956 at Manchester College of Technology in the United Kingdom, where experts cut it into 23 narrow, slightly curved strips, using a circular saw. When finally read and translated it appeared to be a treasure map which gave 64 locations, in Jerusalem and surrounding areas, where an incredible amount of gold and silver was buried. If this is a real treasure map and the treasure is real, we are talking about an estimated 25 tons of gold and 65 tons of silver, according to the experts who calculated this from the scroll text.

Special Attributes

The Copper Scroll is an anomaly for several reasons:

- It is the only copper scroll that has been found; all the others are made of parchment or papyrus.

- It does not fit in with any of the classification systems, as it is not biblical or sectarian, and it is not a literary type of writing.

- It is written in a form of Hebrew different from the form of the rest of the Dead Sea Scrolls. In fact, it is not similar to any Hebrew that we know and may be a local dialect.

- The script is different from the script in the other scrolls and is unique.

- In certain words, spelling is different from what we would expect.

One of the problems with this is that it seems unlikely that the Essenes, an ascetic sect that gave up worldly possessions, would own or be in possession of that much treasure. Many speculate this could be the Temple treasure in Jerusalem that may have been hidden before the Romans entered and destroyed the city in A.D. 66–70. Also, if it was the Temple treasure, why would they give the Qumran sect the map to hide with their scrolls? Many questions are unanswered and speculation abounds.

◀ Not only is the material of the Copper Scroll different, but so too are the language that is used and the subject matter, which is specifically about buried treasure.

Some experts believe that this is just a fictional account and that there never really was any such treasure, in which case the map could be a fictional story of buried treasure. Other well-known experts believe this is a real treasure map and the treasure may be still waiting to be found. The map is very specific in that it indicates the specific locations; that is, tombs, pools, underground, etc., exact amounts of treasure, and the depth of the buried treasure.

▼ It is known that much treasure was taken from the Temple in Jerusalem before its fall to the Romans in A.D. 68, but the exact nature of the treasure and all of the locations are still to be identified.

▲ Present day Jerusalem, showing the city walls and the Al-Aqsa mosque, built on the site of the Temple.

Specifically, the scroll gives a list of three main locations in which most of the treasure is hidden. These locations are Jerusalem, Jericho and its surroundings, and in the Dead Sea area. In addition to gold and silver there are temple vessels, garments of priests, and other temple furnishings. It not only gives the location of the treasure but its exact description, and the exact distance to dig measured in cubits.

The Copper Scroll does not have any introduction or preface. It just begins by listing the treasure and its locations. It describes each treasure location this way:

- It gives the exact location of one of the places of the hidden treasure and how deep it is buried or hidden.

- It describes what the treasure consists of, for example, gold, silver, utensils, garments, etc., and how much is present.

- Seven of the locations end with two or three Greek letters. No one knows what these letters signify.

The last hiding place mentioned, number 64, is said to contain no treasure, but a duplicate of the Copper Scroll that gives further explanations and measurements of the locations of the treasure. Some have speculated that one needs both maps to find the treasure. It is also possible that the second map explains how to decode the first and what the Greek letters may mean.

▲ A view of the Dead Sea. Qumran sits on the hills above the shore at a distance of only a few hundred yards.

▼ The city of Jericho. Qumran is located equidistant from Jerusalem and Jericho, above the Dead Sea.

◄ John Allegro standing in the mouth of one of the caves at Qumran, where he spent so much time.

John Allegro

▲ Here, John Allegro is seen sitting in the scriptorium, where the scribes would have written the scrolls as long as two thousand years before.

One scroll expert, John Allegro, believed the treasure to be real and searched for it. John Allegro was born in London in 1923 and died in February 1988. He wrote numerous books on the scrolls and in 1953 he was recruited as a member of a team to study the scrolls, which he did until 1970. He was one of the more controversial members of the team and challenged the orthodox or traditional views of the scrolls. He was also one of the first to state that the delay in publishing the scrolls was a Vatican conspiracy. He was so convinced that there was a real buried treasure that in 1962 he mounted an expedition to search for this treasure. He looked for documents, artifacts, and just about anything that could give him clues to its whereabouts. Unfortunately, no treasure was uncovered, but many today still believe that in this area of the world a vast amount of treasure still lies waiting for some explorer who can read the secrets written on the Copper Scroll. The one positive accomplishment of his expedition was that he received much media attention and the Dead Sea Scrolls were again in the public arena. King Hussein, who was very interested in this treasure hunt, visited the expedition in 1960. Some of the possible locations have been claimed to be identified but no treasure was found.

Major Questions Posed by the Copper Scroll

The discovery of the Copper Scroll creates one of the greatest challenges to the currently accepted theory that the Essenes at Qumran were the ones responsible for hiding the scrolls in the cave as well as writing some of them. As mentioned previously, it seems that this sect renounced all worldly possessions. It is unlikely that this group of Essenes would have possessed the amount of gold and silver that this scroll indicates so, if the buried treasure is real, where did it come from and who hid it? The fact that the Copper Scroll was hidden in a cave with the Dead Sea Scrolls is a challenge to this theory, unless it can be shown to have been placed there by a different group that was unaware of the Dead Sea Scrolls being hidden in that cave. This would be quite a coincidence but it is still a possibility that the Dead Sea Scrolls and the Copper Scroll could have come from two different sources and could have been hidden in the same location by chance. Or perhaps some group who possessed this treasure asked the Qumran community to hide the map in one of the caves for them. There are many possibilities but few facts.

Some believe that the cache described on the Copper Scroll came from the Temple in Jerusalem and that it was hidden before the temple was sacked and destroyed by the Roman army in A.D. 68. This is a good possibility as the Jerusalem Temple would have been the only source of so much gold and silver at that time. Another clue is that specific temple items and furnishings are described in the treasure list. Some experts believe that the temple priests hid this trove throughout the 64 locations mentioned in the Copper Scroll and made a map on copper so that it could be recovered sometime in the future. Either the priests themselves hid the Copper Scroll in Cave 3 or they asked the Qumran community to hide it for them. One of the problems with this theory is that it appears that the Qumran community did not get along well with the priests at the Jerusalem Temple. It is also interesting to note that the Temple in Jerusalem acted as a bank and many wealthy individuals and merchants used it to store and protect their valuables.

▼ Cave 3, also called the Pillar Cave, where the Copper scroll was found at the rear of the cave.

▲ An artist's impression of the priests who were thought to have hidden the Temple treasure and had the Copper Scroll crafted to keep a record of the hiding places.

The Temple Treasure

Since the amount of gold and silver described appears to be just too much for any one group, even the Jerusalem Temple, to possess, many scroll experts believe this description of the treasure and hiding places was just made up by the author of the Copper Scroll. Why would someone spend the time and money to inscribe a make-believe story on a valuable piece of copper and then hide it in a desert cave? Modern scholars have reevaluated the amount of gold and silver that is listed in the Copper Scroll and believe that the original estimates were in fact way too high. They now believe that it describes only about one third as much gold and silver as was originally calculated. This would put it at a more reasonable amount and would make it consistent with the amount of gold and silver housed in the Jerusalem Temple. In the 1960s, it was calculated that the amount of gold and silver contained in this treasure would be worth over a million dollars.

The Findings Summarised

A major problem with this theory is that these two groups did not like each other and in fact, the Essenes believed the Jerusalem priests were apostate and evil, so why would they help each other? Maybe this is a case of two enemies uniting to fight a more dangerous and common enemy, the Romans.

In the Copper Scroll, there is also the mention of eight different locations in which scrolls have been buried. Are the Dead Sea Scroll caves one of those locations and are the others waiting to be found?

▼ A group of 20th century Samarians seen holding an ornamented scroll which is probably similar to the original Dead Sea Scrolls.

The pieces of the Copper Scroll are housed at the Archeological Museum of Jordan located in Amman. They are displayed in a

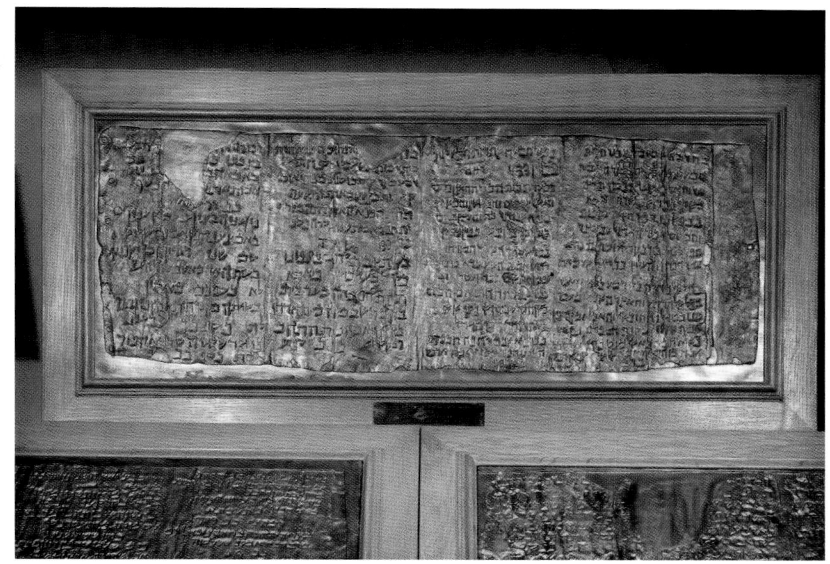

◀ Fragments of the Copper Scroll are housed in the Archeological Museum in Amman, Jordan.

specially designed glass case lined in velvet. Unfortunately, the Copper Scroll continues to oxidize slowly, especially at the places where it was cut by the circular saw. It may eventually disintegrate and disappear altogether if conservation is not successful.

It does not seem likely that this treasure map is just a made-up story. Copper was very expensive, especially the type of very pure copper that was used to make the scroll. Also, the etching process using hammer and chisel would have been a difficult and time-consuming job. Lastly, the locations described are so precise and accurate that it gives the impression of being a real treasure map. If it were a story or a prank, why would someone hide it so securely in a cave so that no one found it for generations or even thousands of years? In addition, the fact that it was written on copper and not parchment or papyrus would indicate that the writer wanted it preserved for a long period of time. In conclusion, all of these facts lead one to believe that it is a real treasure map and the treasure may still be waiting to be discovered.

9 The New Testament and the Dead Sea Scrolls

COMPARISON BETWEEN THE SCROLLS AND THE CANON OF CHRISTIAN TEACHING HAS RAISED MANY QUESTIONS ABOUT THE ASSOCIATION OF JESUS WITH THE COMMUNITY AND ITS TEACHINGS.

Introduction

Upon hearing about the discovery of the Dead Sea Scrolls, many people expected that the information in the scrolls would change our understanding of Judaism, and especially of Christianity. Some even believed, or hoped, it would turn Christianity upside down. As we have mentioned, the Qumran community flourished at the time when, and in the location where, Jesus lived and preached. In fact, Khirbet Qumran is a mere 13 miles from Jerusalem. This was one of the places where Christianity began and this the possibility that the Qumran community knew of Jesus or vice versa.

Scroll texts that may be related to the New Testament can be reconstructed differently depending on the bias of the scholar doing the translation. So, just because one expert interprets

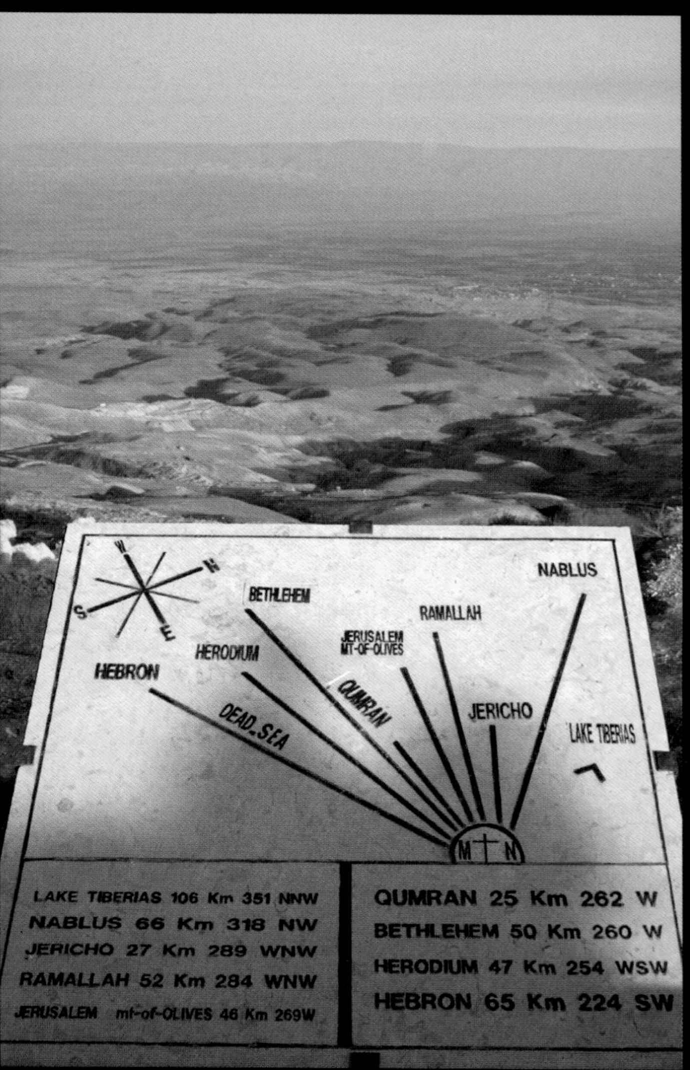

▶ Conspiracy theories abounded regarding the content of some of the Dead Sea Scrolls including accusations that Pope John XXIII was instrumental in trying to prevent their publication.

◀ A directional chart on the summit of Mount Nebo in Jordan showing the distances to key sites including Jerusalem, Jericho, and Qumran.

a text a certain way does not mean that every expert agrees with him. This was certainly the case with the texts that were considered to exhibit New Testament parallels. Anything that would affect religious beliefs of the world, especially Christianity, is threatening and would be very controversial. During the period of time in which the scrolls from Cave 4 were not published and were hidden from the world, conspiracy rumors regarding the Vatican's involvement abounded.

Theories and Conspiracy

In 1991 a book by Michael Baigent and Richard Leigh entitled *The Dead Sea Scrolls Deception* was published. This thrust the Dead Sea Scrolls into the international limelight yet again. In this book, the authors claimed that there was a conspiracy by the Vatican to suppress the information found in some of the scrolls, believing that it challenged the Christian faith. It turns out that there was no conspiracy at all. None of the scrolls or fragments as far as we know was ever destroyed, and there was no cover up or fear from the Vatican regarding the information in the scrolls.

So, in what light did the scrolls portray Christianity, and is there mention of Jesus, John the Baptist, or other early Christian leaders in the texts? Most scroll scholars believe that there are no references to early Christianity, Jesus, or any other early Christian leaders in the scrolls. They believe the similarities between the Dead Sea Scroll authors and Christianity occurs because the writers of the scrolls and the early Christians may have been using the same primary sources to compose their materials. Thus, there could have been a story about a great master healing someone that predated the scrolls and Christianity. The writers of the scrolls might have known about this story and incorporated it into their writings. The same thing happened with the early Christians. When they put their stories about Jesus into writing, they may have incorporated some of these early stories and adapted them to Jesus, so the similarities are thought to be due to a common source and not necessarily caused by borrowing ideas from each other. This is the consensus of most scroll scholars but not everyone agrees. More research needs to be done and more possibilities need to be explored.

▶ The scrolls make mention of a great master with healing powers, which some have taken as a direct reference to Jesus.

It appears that the general public view scholars as being almost infallible. They do not realize that these scholars do not always work with undisputable facts but make many assumptions and guesses. Sometimes scholars have a bias to their own theories and may shape the data to fit their conceptions. They may miss some new insight or new way of looking at the data. This, I believe, is also the case with the Dead Sea Scrolls' researchers. Many of the fragments are badly damaged and the letters are hard to make out. The experts try to figure out what these words and sentences say and many times this is just a guess. Errors do occur in their judgment.

The Complexities of Language

Other factors add to this confusion. Because the Hebrew language does not contain vowels, only consonants, it makes it more difficult to guess what words the consonants may represent. Anyone trying to figure out a word could interpret it to mean many different things, as there are many words that begin and end with the same consonants but have different meanings. So, to determine what the actual word is using just consonants is much guesswork and extrapolation. When reading a text you have to guess by trying to figure out what the sentence meant and eliminating which words would not fit the sense. Thus, a translator might read into these incomplete fragments and consonants the meaning he or she wanted to convey. It would be posible to pick the words more consistent with a particular bias. We must be careful to realize that this process of recovering the letters on the scrolls is very subjective, and not always correct.

▶ Cave 7 in the Qumran complex, where some particularly interesting fragments have been found.

The Jesus Connection

Are there scroll fragments that refer to Jesus and early Christianity? The answer is that there are candidates for this We will look at several of the more interesting texts in the Dead Sea Scrolls that are the most controversial regarding early Christianity and Jesus.

An interesting text fragment was recovered from Cave 7. Fragment 7Q5 (recall that the number preceding the letter Q refers to the cave number), is alleged to be a New Testament text. Some experts concluded that it was the story of Jesus walking on water. This story is in the bible in Mark 6:52–53. It reads as follows:

… for they did not understand about the loaves, but their hearts were hardened. When they had crossed over, they came to land at Gennesaret and moored to the shore.

The Dead Sea Scrolls 7Q5 version is as follows:

… understood about the loaves; their hearts were hardened. And when they had crossed over, they landed at Gennesaret, and anchored there. And when they got …

▼ Some experts have suggested that one of the Cave 7 fragments relates to the story of Jesus walking on water, which is contained in St Mark's Gospel.

There is a strong similarity within just these few sentences. This reconstruction of the Dead Sea Scrolls text was advocated by Peter Carsten, who claimed that this was evidence of the New Testament being represented in the scrolls. The critics of his translation base their disagreement on how he reconstructed the text. They accuse him of making many assumptions as to what the words should have been and claim that it could have been intepreted in a different way.

Another example is the famous Slain or Pierced Messiah text. Does this text actually describe Jesus and his violent execution? Here is what 4Q285 says:

Isaiah the prophet: [The thickets of the forest] will be cut [down with an axe and Lebanon by a majestic one will f]all. And there shall come forth a shoot from the stump of Jesse [...] the Branch of David and they will enter into judgment with [...] and the Prince of the Congregation, the Br[anch of David] will kill him [... by strok]es and by wounds. And a Priest [of renown (?)] will command [... the s]lai[n] of the Kitti[m ...]

▼ One of the fragments from cave 7 which, it has been suggested, constitute part of a New Testament text.

Some scholars believe that this text describes a slain and dying messiah. Could this be a reference to Jesus Christ? The debate continues. Unfortunately, the sections of the scrolls that contain these possible New Testament texts are badly mutilated and no clear conclusion can be drawn. In fact, other translators interpret the above text as actually saying that the Prince will do the killing and not be killed. So, you can see that there are varied opinions from different experts concerning what the text actually says.

◄ The familiar Christian image of the crucifixion, which bears a strong similarity to references to a slain or pierced messiah that can be found in the Dead Sea Scrolls.

▲ Contrasting images of Jesus, who has been identified by some as the scrolls' Teacher of Righteousness, and Paul, the scrolls' Wicked Priest, as depicted in these early 20th-century paintings.

The Teacher of Righteousness and The Wicked Priest

Two individuals that are mentioned in the scrolls and who play a prominent role are the Teacher of Righteousness, who is good, and the Wicked Priest who, of course, is evil. This Wicked Priest goes by many different designations in the scrolls; The Preacher of Lies, The Scoffer, and the Liar. Several different New Testament figures have been suggested to be the Teacher of Righteousness. These candidates include Jesus, John the Baptist, and even James, the brother of Jesus. It has been speculated that The Wicked Priest is the apostle Paul and one scholar even believes the Wicked Priest to be Jesus. It is very interesting that the scrolls tell us very little about this mysterious person called The Teacher of Righteousness. They do not tell us his name, what he looks like, where he was born, how he became the founder of the sect, etc., so this is a man of mystery and this is an area that is still being studied and researched. Historians and scholars continue to debate the meaning and translation of many of these passages. Let us look at some additional examples.

Further Parallels with Jesus

Scroll 4Q242 is known as the Prayer of Nabonidus or The Healing of King Nabonidus. It has a strong parallel to the New Testament story of Jesus healing the paralytic and forgiving his sins. There are two different versions of this tale in the Gospels, one in Matthew 9:1 and the other in Mark 2:1. The story goes as follows: There was a paralytic who was brought to Jesus on a mat, since he could not walk of his own accord. In the version in Matthew, it is stated that he was just brought to Jesus, but in the version in Mark, this occurred in Capernaum and the paralytic was lowered through the roof since they could not get near Jesus due to the crowds. Four men carried this paralytic and when they arrived at the house where Jesus was,

▼ The image of Jesus as a healer of the sick and dying has similarities with the healing stories contained in the scrolls and particularly with the healing of King Nabonidus.

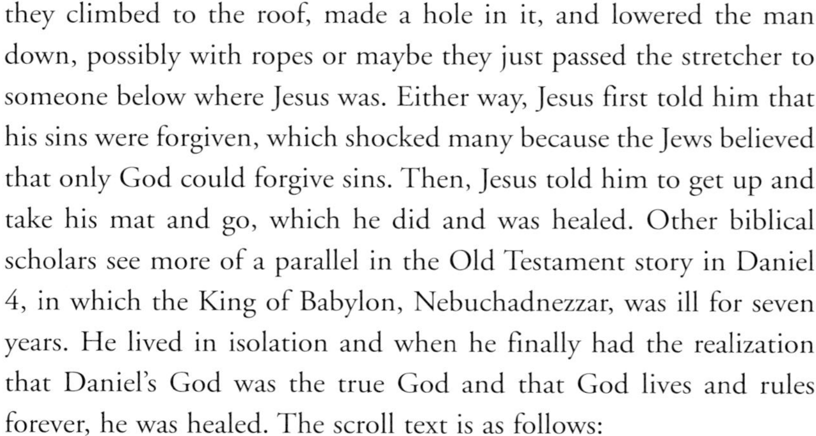

they climbed to the roof, made a hole in it, and lowered the man down, possibly with ropes or maybe they just passed the stretcher to someone below where Jesus was. Either way, Jesus first told him that his sins were forgiven, which shocked many because the Jews believed that only God could forgive sins. Then, Jesus told him to get up and take his mat and go, which he did and was healed. Other biblical scholars see more of a parallel in the Old Testament story in Daniel 4, in which the King of Babylon, Nebuchadnezzar, was ill for seven years. He lived in isolation and when he finally had the realization that Daniel's God was the true God and that God lives and rules forever, he was healed. The scroll text is as follows:

▼ In an early 20th-century painting, Nebuchadnezzar is depicted being healed when he accepts the true God of Daniel.

The words of the prayer of Nabonidus, king of Babylonia, the great king, when he was smitten with a severe inflammation at the command of God, in Teima.

I, Nabonidus, was smitten with a severe inflammation lasting seven years. Because I was thus changed, becoming like a beast, I prayed to the Most High and he forgave my sins. An exorcist—a Jew, in fact, a member of the community of exiles—came to me and said, "Declare and write down this story, and so ascribe glory and greatness to the name of God Most High." Accordingly, I have myself written it down. I was smitten with a severe inflammation while in Teima, by the command of God Most High. Then for seven years I continued praying to the gods made of silver and gold, bronze, iron, wood, stone and clay, for I used to think that they really were Gods.

▲ A basalt stele on which is carved the figure of Nabonidus, found in Babylon in southern Iraq, and thought to date from the fifth century B.C.

So, you can see the strong parallels here between this story and the Gospel story of Jesus healing the paralytic.

Why are these stories so similar? There are several possibilities. Was this story of Jesus healing the paralytic actually the same story told in a different manner? Was the exorcist Jew actually Jesus? Jesus would have been looked at as an exile at that time, so some believe this is evidence that the Qumran community knew of Jesus and his miracles. Others think the reverse. Maybe the New Testament writers, who knew of the Essenes and their writings, adopted this story from them years later and applied it to Jesus, changing around some of the details. Let us look at another story with New Testament parallels.

Known as the "Resurrection fragment" or "Redemption and Resurrection" or the "Messianic Apocalypse," this story talks about a messiah who will rule the heavens and the earth, the resurrection of the dead, and has parallels with the Gospels regarding the signs of the Messiah. It reads as follows:

[the hea]vens and the earth will listen to His Messiah, and none therein will stray from the commandments of the holy ones. Seekers of the Lord, strengthen yourselves in His service! All you hopeful in (your) heart, will you not find the Lord in this?

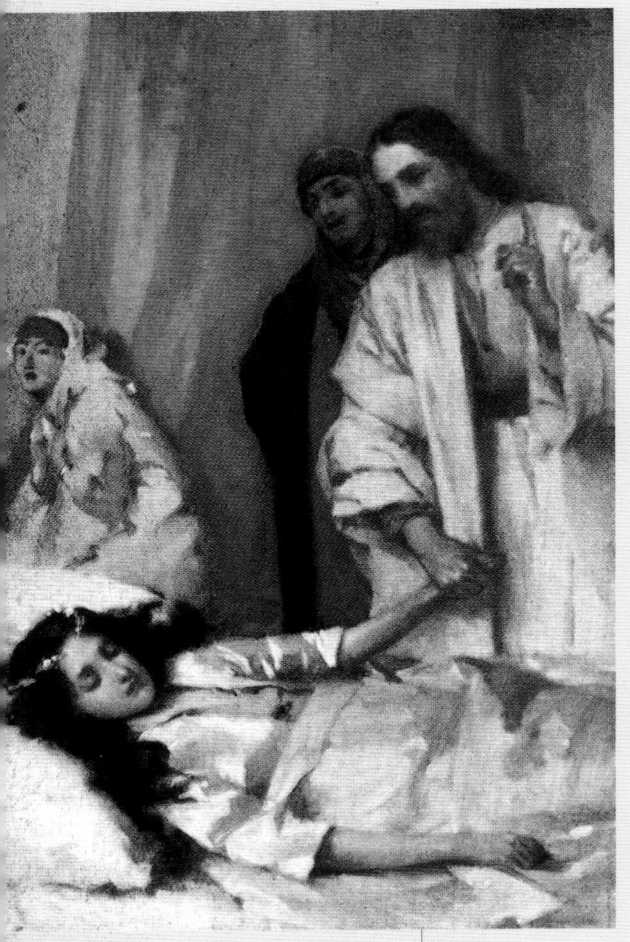

For the Lord will consider the pious *(hasidim)* and call the righteous by name. Over the poor His spirit will hover and will renew the faithful with His power. And He will glorify the pious on the throne of the eternal Kingdom. He who liberates the captives, restores sight to the blind, straightens the b[ent] And f[or] ever I will clea[ve to the h]opeful and in His mercy . . . And the fr[uit . . .] will not be delayed for anyone. And the Lord will accomplish glorious things which have never been as [He . . .] *For He will heal the wounded, and revive the dead and bring good news to the poor* . . . He will lead the uprooted and knowledge . . . and smoke (?)
(Michael O. Wise, translation)

This text includes the themes of healing the blind and the wounded, liberating the captives, straightening the bent, reviving the dead, etc. This is the eschatological theme from the New Testament, and is similar to Jesus' words in Luke 11:20 and Matthew 11:4–5 (NKJV):

▲ The New Testament story of the raising of Jairus's daughter shows distinct similarities to scroll references to a messiah with the power of reviving the dead.

But if I cast out demons with the finger of God, surely the kingdom of God has come upon you.
Luke 11:20

Go and tell John the things which you hear and see: The blind see and the lame walk; the lepers are cleansed and the deaf hear; the dead are raised up and the poor have the gospel preached to them.
Matthew 11:4–5 (NKJV)

◄ Further references in the New Testament about healing the blind, the sick and the lame all find parallels within certain of The Dead Sea Scrolls texts.

Key Christian Teachings

There are many similarities between the teachings of Jesus and the texts of the scrolls. These include the idea of diseases being caused by demons or evil spirits, removing the demon by exorcism just like Jesus did, and even a similarity between the beatitudes of Jesus and the scroll texts. This section, 4QBeat, has similar statements to the beatitudes.

Matthew 5:3–11

The Beatitudes

2 And he opened his mouth and taught them, saying:
3 "Blessed are the poor in spirit, for theirs is the kingdom of heaven.
4 "Blessed are those who mourn, for they shall be comforted.
5 "Blessed are the meek, for they shall inherit the earth.
6 "Blessed are those who hunger and thirst for righteousness, for they shall be satisfied.
7 "Blessed are the merciful, for they shall receive mercy.
8 "Blessed are the pure in heart, for they shall see God.
9 "Blessed are the peacemakers, for they shall be called sons of God.
10 "Blessed are those who are persecuted for righteousness' sake, for theirs is the kingdom of heaven.
11 "Blessed are you when others revile you and persecute you and utter all kinds of evil against you falsely on my account.
12 "Rejoice and be glad, for your reward is great in heaven, for so they persecuted the prophets who were before you."

Cave 4 Fragment

Blessed are those who hold to her (Wisdom's) precepts
and do not hold to the ways of iniquity.
Blessed are those who rejoice in her,
and do not burst forth in ways of folly.

◀ A 15th-century Italian painting shows Jesus preaching the Sermon on the Mount, a core Christian teaching which closely echoes the text of one of the Cave 4 fragments.

**Blessed are those who seek her with pure hands
and do not pursue her with a treacherous heart.
Blessed is the man who has attained Wisdom
and walks in the Law of the Most High.**

It seems that circumstantial evidence would point strongly to the possibility of the Qumran community hearing about or even knowing Jesus. In fact, many have speculated that John the Baptist may have been raised by the Qumran community and was even a member. If this had been the case, it would probably point to Jesus having some interaction with that community. In addition, the proximity of Jesus and the early Christians, and the dates in which Jesus lived, overlap with the existence of the community and would point strongly to their association. Also, they both appeared to be rebels from the conventional religious ideas of the time. Since they had many views in common and may have influenced each other, it would not be surprising if the Qumran community recorded some of the events associated with these early Christians, especially Jesus. That is what was recorded in those fragments. Further restoration and computer recognition of the words on these fragments needs to be done before any definitive conclusion can be drawn.

▼ A depiction of the young John the Baptist, whom it has been speculated was raised in the Qumran community and was even a member.

At the time of Jesus a single faith or doctrine did not exist for the Jews. There were many variations on Judaism and not one creed. This is reflected in the library at Qumran where there is not just one religious theme in their library of scrolls, but a cross section of many ideas, doctrines, and beliefs prevalent at that time. Therefore, we need to look at this collection as a library of the different

◀ An apocalyptic view of a New Jerusalem, which can be found in views of the end time in both the New Testament Book of Revelation and the Dead Sea Scrolls, when the good will prevail over the evil ones.

thoughts, beliefs, and practices that obtained. There are some strong common themes that link Christian beliefs with what has been discovered in some of the texts of the Dead Sea scrolls. There is the expectation that a messiah would appear and that there would be an apocalyptic end time with evil being conquered by good. We will look more closely at some of the similarities between the New Testament and the Dead Sea Scrolls in the next chapter.

The End Time

Most are familiar with the end time scenario in the New Testament book of Revelation. This apocalyptic description is concerned with the time of tribulation when the evil ones reign over the world; the coming of the Messiah to destroy the evil ones and vindicate the righteous; the dawning of a new era for the victorious believers and the appearance of a new heaven and a new earth. The Dead Sea Scrolls has a similar scenario and it even ends with the belief that the Temple in Jerusalem will be rebuilt or, even more spectacular, that a heavenly Jerusalem will come down from heaven. It was believed by scholars, before the discovery of the Dead Sea Scrolls, that this Christian apocalypse of the end times was unique to Christianity. Since we find such a similar description of this in the Dead Sea Scrolls, that assumption cannot be correct. There are differences, but there is no question that the same themes and ideas are expounded in each. So it appears that this belief in an apocalyptic end time did not originate with Christianity, but predates it, as revealed in the Dead Sea Scrolls.

The Coming of the Messiah

In the Dead Sea Scrolls there is mention of a belief in the coming of a prophet who precedes the Messiah and heralds his coming. In the Bible, this is John the Baptist, but some scholars believe that the Qumran community knew of John the Baptist and may have been referring to him in the scrolls. He does meet much of the scrolls' description of this prophet and it is believed that he did baptize in the Jordan River several miles north of the Qumran site. It seems very likely that he knew of the Qumran sect and they knew of him. Some even believe he was a member and may have been raised by the sect. The idea of baptism was central to the belief of the Qumran community and also to the teachings of John the Baptist, so it is possible that there

◀ The idea of a prophet who precedes the Messiah is common both to the Bible and the Dead Sea Scrolls, and Baptism was an idea common both to the Essene community and to the followers of Jesus. Here John the Baptist is depicted baptising Jesus in the Jordan river.

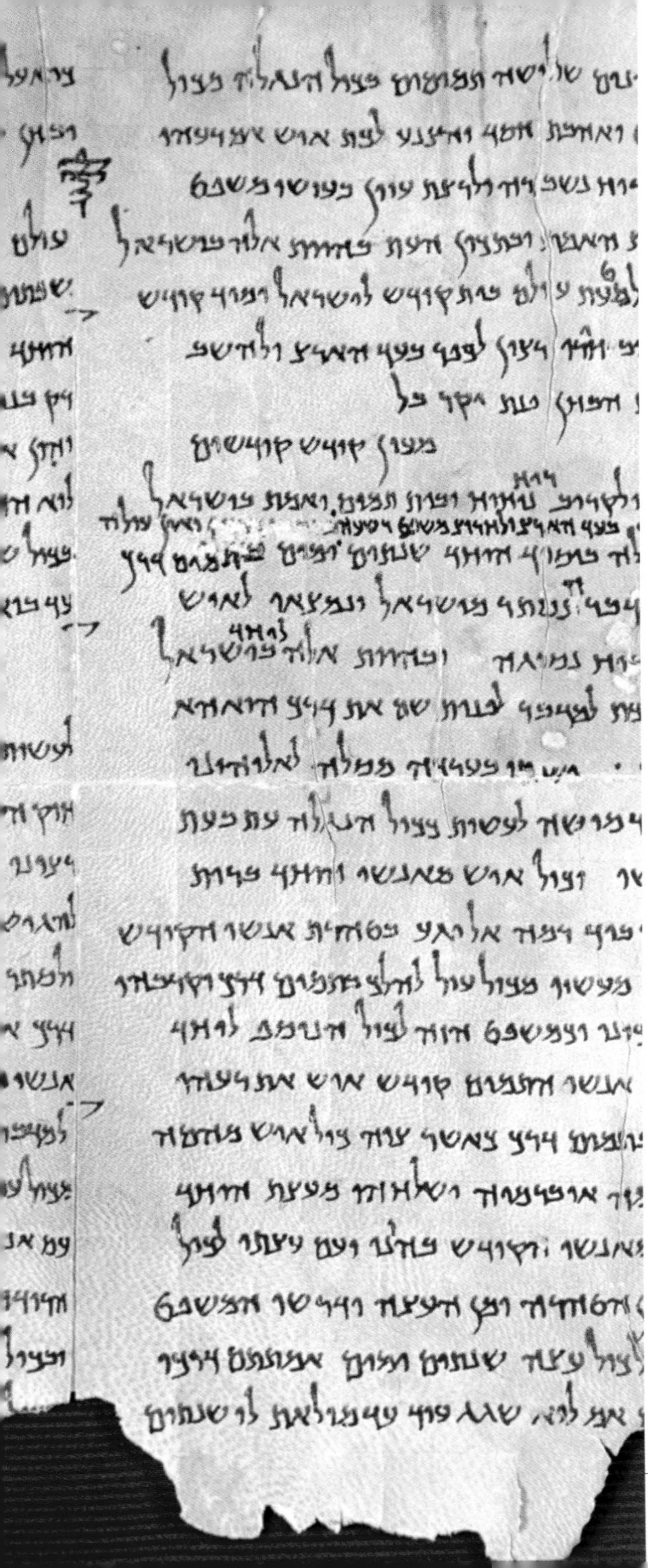

is a definite New Testament correlation between the two. The other possible connection between the Qumran and the New Testament is with the fragments found in Cave 7. These few fragments were written in Greek and were thought to be a section from the Gospel of Mark and other New Testament texts. There is much debate over this and most experts refute this claim. They do not think that these fragments refer to the Gospels, but there is much similarity between the Qumran beliefs and those of the early Christians. In fact, two important and well-known scroll researchers, Robert Eisenman and Barbara Thiering, believe they were identical; that is, the Qumran sect was part of the early Christian community. That was a revolutionary idea in scroll scholarship when first voiced but evidence may be mounting in favor of it. There are just too many inconsistencies to conclude that this group living at Khirbet Qumran by the Dead Sea was the Essenes mentioned by the ancient writers Josephus, Pliny the Elder, and Philo. At present, few scroll researchers go along with this view, but I think the tide will start to change.

A summary of similarities between the practices mentioned in the Dead Sea Scrolls and those of early Christianity is given opposite.

◄ The Rule of Congregation which contains strong similarities with Christian ritual.

Both:

- Believed and practiced a form of ritual baptism.
- Entertained the idea of two forces, good and evil in conflict, both in heaven and on earth. They both view this as the theme of light and darkness.
- Believed in an eschatological end time in which good would prevail over evil.
- Believed in the coming of a messiah (two for the Qumran community as opposed to one messiah for the Christian community).
- Had sacred meals which involved bread and wine.

This last similarity is very interesting. It was actually only to be eaten by those who were ritually pure. If we look at Rule of the Congregation this is what it says about the sacred meal:

When they meet at the communal table, to set out bread and wine, and the communal table is arranged to eat and to drink, no one shall extend his hand to the first portion of the bread and the wine before the priest. For he shall bless the first portion of the bread and the wine and shall extend his hand to the bread first. Afterwards, the messiah of Israel shall extend his hands to the bread. Afterwards, all of the congregation of the community shall bless each according to his importance. They shall act according to this statute whenever the meal is arranged when as many as ten meet together.

Did Jesus borrow ideas from the community, was there in fact a common source, or did they evolve independently?

10 Messianic Ideas and Jesus in the Dead Sea Scrolls

COUNTLESS QUESTIONS STILL REMAIN UNANSWERED, NOT LEAST ABOUT THE IDENTITY OF THE LAY MESSIAH AND HIS SPIRITUAL COUNTERPART, THE TEACHER OF RIGHTEOUSNESS.

nicium sancti
euuangelij secũ
dum iohanne

n principio erat
uerbum et uerbũ
erat apud deum

Introduction

▲ The written word was fundamental to Judaism at the time that the scrolls were compiled, and remains so today. Here, in an early 20th-century painting, two priests are seen reading a scroll and debating its meaning.

▶ There continues to be speculation amongst academics about the "Teacher of Righteousness" in the Dead Sea Scrolls, with some suggesting that it is a clear reference to Jesus.

The Dead Sea Scrolls state that the founder of their sect was called the "Teacher of Righteousness" and that he was put to death. Members of the sect believed that in the last days or end time there would be the coming of not one, but two different messiahs. One of these messiahs was also called the Teacher of Righteousness. Is it possible that they believed this coming messiah would be the same person as the founder of their sect who was killed? If so, does this mean that they believed he would be resurrected at the end time to lead them in battle and to final victory against the evil ones? This messiah was the "Priestly Messiah" or "Anointed One." The other messiah, who would also appear at the end time, is referred to as the Lay Messiah. He would be a descendent of King David. Thus, the idea of two messiahs appearing at the end time is different from the New Testament view of only one Messiah, Jesus, appearing at his second coming. The two messiahs mentioned in the Dead Sea Scrolls would unite and work together. The Teacher of Righteousness would wield the spiritual powers and the Lay Messiah would wield the secular powers.

The Lay Messiah or Davidic Messiah would in a sense be a warrior messiah as he would lead the battle against evil and restore the Kingdom of God on earth. This messiah is similar to the Christian Messiah, Jesus, who, according to the New Testament, will return as the conquering lion, defeat evil, restore the kingdom of God, and bring in the heavenly Jerusalem. The roles of the two messiahs of the Qumran community seem, to some extent, to be combined in the person of Jesus.

The True Messiah

Some have asked if the Teacher of Righteousness mentioned in the Dead Sea Scrolls could be a reference to Jesus. Most experts think this is unlikely, as these texts were probably written before the time of Jesus (based on C14 tests) and the similarity is probably due to common ideas of the Messiah that both groups may have had. There may have been a common tradition that both groups borrowed from. These questions are still being raised and debated among scroll scholars.

▼ A fragment of the scroll of the prophet Ezekiel, which is held at the Rockefeller Museum in Jerusalem.

Some have looked for similarities between the Qumran community and the early Christians. Although there are similarities, there are also major differences. For example, the people of the Qumran community practiced separatism from the world, whereas Jesus preached to everyone including the wine drinkers and gluttons. Jesus and early Christianity never wanted to restrict their membership and doctrines to just a few but to spread it to everyone over the entire world. Also, the Qumran community never refer to their Teacher of Righteousness as the risen Lord or to being one with God. This seems to be unique to Christianity.

This would lead to the conclusion that there was no interaction or contact between these two groups. However, it is important to bear in mind that the C14 dating was done on only a few selected scroll fragments. The results indicate that the date of the scrolls that were tested was between 200 B.C. and

◄ A scholar from the Jerusalem Israel Antiquities Authority takes a piece of scroll for carbon dating in 1976.

A.D. 100. But it is accepted that there is a margin of error of 50–100 years and also, it is only an indication of when the animal whose skins were used actually died; that is, stopped breathing and had no more intake of C14, and not when the scrolls were actually written. It is possible that the scribes used skins of animals that had died many years before; just as we may have a stock of paper, they may have had a stock of animal skins. Sampling could be another factor; very few scroll samples were tested and possibly, some of the ones that were not tested are more recent; that is, closer to A.D. 70.

So, carbon dating cannot rule out the possibility that some of the scrolls were written at the time of Jesus or John the Baptist, or even later. Also, even if the Qumran community did not write about Jesus or John, that does not necessarily mean they did not have any contact with each other. It is possible they did not have time or get around to writing about this before A.D. 68, when the Romans destroyed their community.

There is something even more compelling to suggest that there was contact between these two groups. Even though there are differences, the similarities of important beliefs such as baptism, the sacredness of the meal, and the concept of the end time are much too strong to ignore. Also, the proximity of the Christians and the Qumran site, and even the location of the Jordan River, used in baptismal rites by John, cannot be ignored. Most importantly, the Qumran community

▶ The concept of Jesus as the son of God is unique to Christianity and is depicted here in the 15th-century painting of Christ Glorified in the Court of Heaven.

are more similar to the early Christians than to any other group. Neither the Qumran community nor the early Christians liked the scribes and the Pharisees of the Jerusalem Temple and it could be that they sought alliance, or at least a friendship, with each other.

We do not have sufficient information to be able to come to a definitive conclusion as to whether or not the texts in the Dead Sea Scrolls are directly linked to Christianity and the belief that Jesus was the Son of God who rose from the dead. Perhaps additional scrolls or artifacts will be uncovered in the future which will help to shed more light upon this important question.

Reference

Glossary

Angelic Invocation – The spiritual practice of appealing to angels to intercede in the life of humans, a mystical experience which has seen a resurgence in recent times.

Antichrist – A concept which appears both in Christianity and Islam, and which prophesies the arrival of the false Messiah, whose appearance on earth presages the end of the world and the Last Judgement.

Book of Revelation – The last canonical book of the New Testament in the Bible. It is the only biblical book that is wholly composed of apocalyptic literature.

Buddhism – The philosophy associated with the teachings of Shakyamuni, the Buddha, who lived in India in the sixth to fifth century B.C. Central to its teachings are the four Noble Truths, although there are many similarities in its code of conduct with the Ten Commandments of the Old Testament.

Cathars – Dualist gnostic 12th-13th century heretics who challenged existing medieval church doctrine more than any other contemporary movement. Particularly strong in southern France and northern Italy, the Cathars held the dualist belief that the earthly, physical world was evil, and that humans are therefore "trapped" in a material prison of the body. Their allowing women as well as men in their priesthood, a fervent belief that the existing church was merely corrupt, evil, and power-hungry, their powerful healing tradition, vegetarian diet and ascetic lifestyle coupled with a strong willingness to die for their beliefs no matter what the circumstances, placed them at odds with the church and led to their persecution and a major Inquisition against them.

Crusades – A series of wars undertaken by various European Christian nations between A.D. 1096 and A.D. 1291 and sanctioned by the papacy, their intention being to free the Holy Land (Palestine) from Muslim rule.

Divination – The use of magic or esoteric practices, including Astrology, to discover information not normally accessible to humankind. Divinatory practices can be found in many religions, but not Christianity, which is generally opposed to them.

Gnosis – Gnosis is a Greek term meaning 'knowledge' or 'wisdom,' especially that of a directly inspired, intuitive nature as opposed to that obtained using a purely intellectual approach focusing only on external doctrine or analysis. In general, it might be better understood today as a profound inner experience, and/or as a continuing process of personal 'revelation,' whereby one seeks union with God or the Infinite, and to know the reality behind the Reality. In the early centuries of Christianity, there was a great variety of groups identifying themselves as 'gnostic.' Gnostics on the whole placed a high premium on individual experience and revelation and a greater appreciation of the feminine, understandably leading to serious clashes with orthodoxy.

'Gnostic gospels' – Modern-day parlance for the important texts found in Egypt at Nag Hammadi in 1945 and published in 1977. Although many ancient Christian texts have long been identified as 'gnostic' in nature and have been criticized, studied, burned, or esteemed for centuries, today they are considered to be early non-canonical texts or apocryphal texts about the life of Jesus, i.e., outside the accepted church canon, and thus remain as controversial as they are fascinating to many. Two of the key gnostic gospels, highlighting Mary Magdalene in particular, include The Gospel of Mary and The Gospel of Philip.

Hinduism – A term used to describe the beliefs and religious practices of Hindus, which range from village goddess cults to modern gurus. At the heart of all is Moksha, the release from the round of repeated birth and death, which popularized the theory of Karma.

James, the brother of Jesus – Said to have led the post-crucifixion church in Palestine, he has been associated by recent scholars with The Teacher of Righteousness, the spiritual leader of the Essene sect. In medieval times, he was associated with the church of Santiago de Compostela in Spain, one of the most important pilgrimage destinations.

John the Baptist – As precursor of Jesus, whom he baptized, he was a religious leader in his own right. Born into a humble priestly family, he launched a preaching campaign calling for repentance and simple living in anticipation of the 'Coming One.' His popularity created suspicion amongst the authorities, and he was imprisoned by Herod Antipas, and later put to death. He has been associated with the Essene sect.

Knights Templar – The famed Order of the Temple (A.D. 1119-1312) was a medieval military religious order that existed during the time of the Crusades. Arguably the largest, wealthiest, and most powerful organization outside of the church in the Western world at the time, the Templars were dedicated monastic warriors, bankers to kings, trusted diplomats, farmers, transporters and protectors of pilgrims, business scions, navigators, and more. At its height, their empire consisted of over two thousand commandaries in Europe alone, with more in the Holy Land. Popular and greatly respected for their many victories in battle, inevitably their immense wealth and power became the envy of many, including the French king. In 1307, the leading knights were arrested and accused of many charges, initially only in France, and then in other countries as well. After seven years of brutal imprisonment, torture, and a series of lurid trials, the Order was finally officially suppressed by papal bull in A.D. 1312, although the Pope's final verdict of the charges was as a whole, 'not proven.'

Maccabees – The followers of Judah Maccabee who in 167 B.C. defeated the Seleucids, and entered and cleansed the Temple. This event is celebrated to this day in the Jewish festival of Hanukkah.

Messiah – A concept of Jewish doctrine, which refers to the appointed one of God, who will come at some future time at the beginning of the Messianic age. Throughout history, the Messianic hope has sustained Jews in times of suffering and persecution.

Pliny the Elder – Gaius Plinius Secundus, who lived from A.D. 23 until A.D. 79, was a Roman author, naturalist, and natural philosopher. A considerable military commander, he wrote widely of the many peoples and places that he came across in his travels.

Pharisees – Devout followers of the Jewish tradition who were strongly opposed Roman although they were not active in their opposition to it. The coming of a Messiah was fundamental to their beliefs.

Sadducees – A religious sect who existed in Palestine between 150 B.C. and A.D. 70, they were theologically conservative and were opposed to the Jerusalem church, not least because of their rejection of the concept of resurrection.

Sanskrit – The classical holy language of India, Sanskrit dates back to at least 1,500 B.C. and has a rich tradition of poetry, and scientific and religious texts. It is still used today in Hindu religious rituals.

Teacher of Righteousness – A key figure, who is most prominent in the Damascus document, but whose true identity remains a mystery. Amongst others, he has been associated with James, the brother of Jesus, leader of the post-crucifixion church, and by some, with Jesus himself.

Torah – Comprising the first five books of the Hebrew Bible – Genesis, Exodus, Leviticus, Numbers and Deuteronomy of the Old Testament – scrolls of which are still housed in a tabernacle in every synagogue.

Bibliography

Allegro, John. *The Dead Sea Scrolls, A Reappraisal.* Pelican Books, 1964.

Campbell, Jonathan G. *Dead Sea Scrolls, The Complete Story.* Ulysses Press, 1998.

Davies, A. Powell. *The Meaning of the Dead Sea Scrolls.* Mentor Books, 1956.

De Hamel, Christopher. *The Book. A History of the Bible.* Phaidon, 2001.

Eisenman, Robert. *The Dead Sea Scrolls and the First Christians.* Castle Books, 2006.

Eisenman, Robert, and Wise, Michael. *The Dead Sea Scrolls Uncovered.* Barnes and Noble, 1994.

Gaster, Theodor H., *The Dead Sea Scriptures in English Translation.* Doubleday Anchor Books, 1956.

Hanson, Kenneth. *Dead Sea Scrolls: The Untold Story.* Council Oak books, 1997.

Hodge, Stephen. *The Dead Sea Scrolls Rediscovered.* Seastone, 2003.

Le Loup, J-Y, *The Gospel of Philip*, Rochester, VT: Inner Traditions, 2004

Le Loup, J-Y, *The Gospel of Mary Magdalene*, Rochester, VT: Inner Traditions, 2002

Lim, Timothy H. *The Dead Sea Scrolls, A Very Short Introduction.* Oxford, 2005.

Martinez, Florentino Garcia. *The Dead Sea Scrolls Translated.* Brill and Eerdmans, 1996.

Scrolls from the Dead Sea, An Exhibition of Scrolls and Archeological Artifacts from the Collections of the Israel Antiquities Authority. George Braziller, 1993.

Shanks, Hershel, *Understanding the Dead Sea Scrolls.* Vintage, 1993.

Silberman, Neil Asher. *The Hidden Scrolls, Christianity, Judaism, and the War for the Dead Sea Scrolls.* Grosset/Putnam, 1994.

Vermes, Geza. *The Complete Dead Sea Scrolls in English.* Penguin Books, 1997.

Wise, Michael, Abegg, Martin Jr., and Cook, Edward. *The Dead Sea Scrolls, A New Translation.* HarperCollins, 2005.

Articles

"Bulletin of the American Schools of Oriental Research." *Number 110.* April, 1948. p2-3.

The Biblical Archaeologist. *Volume XI, No. 2.* May, 1948. p21-23.

Text credits

► Archaeologist Yigael Yadin sits in his study at home working on the Temple Scroll.

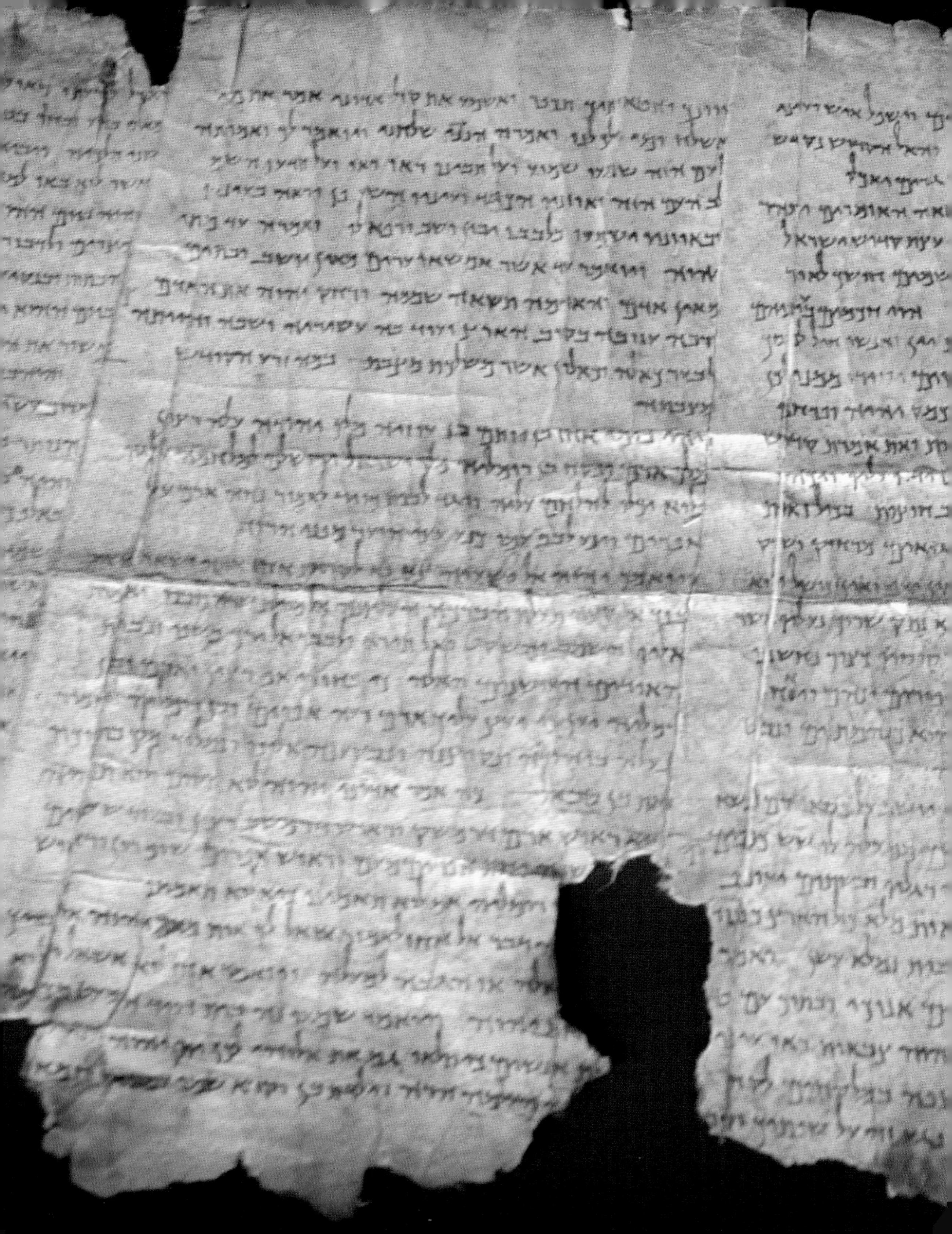

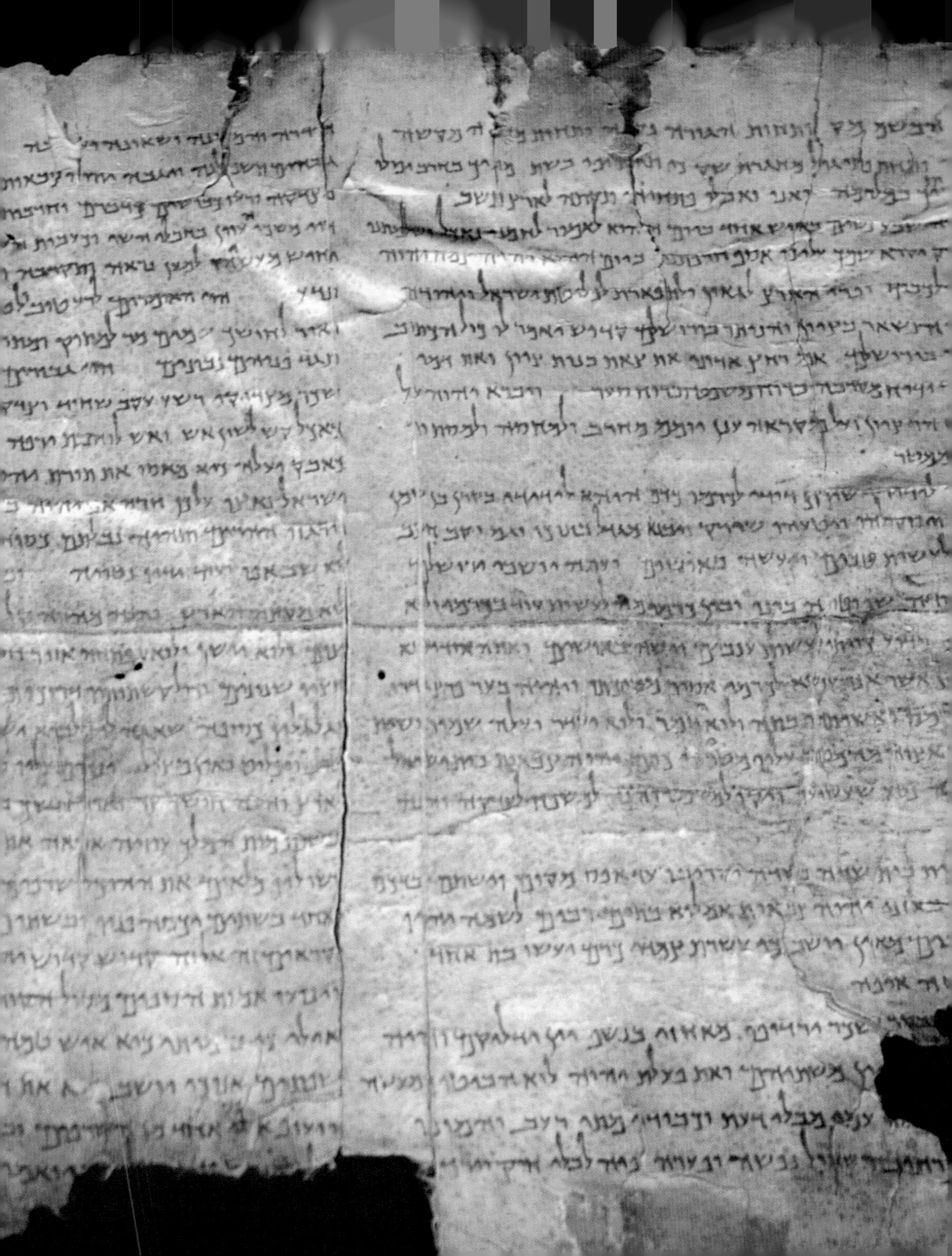

Index

◀ The Great Isaiah Scroll at the Shrine of the Book, in Jerusalem.

R

S

T

U

V

W

Y

Z